Rape: Weapon of War and Mass Destruction

Author: Shabbir H M Tankiwala

Chapter 1

When two elephants fight, it is the grass that suffers. So, as there is an age old saying, "it's a Man's world," so, in patriarchal society when men fights among themselves it's the women who suffers the most.

We humans have seen and been through many ages "Ice-age, Stone-age, Neolithic-age, and now in modern times when we're living in the' Digital age." Lots have change, but, the gender inequality still persist, the female gender are still deprived of certain basic civil rights and liberties, not yet given equal social status in the society, as yet, sexual harassment against women is not condemn as loudly as it should be.

From women's perspective, a woman's most valuable asset is her **Vagina**, but when this precious asset is torn apart by a voracious man, when a man to soothe his mind and for fulfilment of his desire of indulging in sexual fantasy forcefully sucks in his Peni into woman's vagina, what a horrible incident that proves to be for that hapless woman who suffers such excruciating pain, one can only imagine.

A woman who gets raped, have to, for rest her of the life live with taboo and stigma. The effects are deep and long lasting.

This post-traumatic stress can manifest itself in nightmares or flashbacks, where the woman feels she is once again experiencing the attack. "She can smell the alcohol on the breath of the rapist and it doesn't feel as if it is happening years ago.

Sexual violence has been employed as a strategic weapon of war for at least as long as historians have been documenting conflicts. Indeed, members of nearly every standing army in history have participated in some form of rape warfare.

Indeed, sexual deprivation and base desire cannot explain why even educated military strategists would advocate the use of sexual violence in warfare.

Article title "Ancient times until World War2" stated: In ancient times: The Hebrew Scriptures (Old Testament) describe the rape of the women of conquered tribes as a routine act. Foreign women were often kidnapped as spoils of war, and either murdered or forced to marry their captors/rapists. This was probably typical behaviour in the Middle-East during Old Testament times. At the time, rape was considered to be a crime against the victim's father or spouse—whoever owned her. Numbers 31:1-18 describes how the army of the ancient Israelites killed every adult Midianite male in battle. Moses then ordered the slaughter in cold blood of most of the captives, including all of the male children who numbered about 32,000. Only the lives of 32,000 women - all virgins -- were spared. Some of the latter were given to the priests as slaves. Most were taken by the Israeli soldiers as captives of war.

More modern times: random cases of rape: Random rape by soldiers during wartime has been a common phenomenon, particularly when there has been a lack of army discipline. UNICEF writes: "From [recent] conflicts in Bosnia and Herzegovina to Peru to Rwanda, girls and women have been singled out for rape, imprisonment, torture and execution. Rape, identified by psychologists as the most intrusive of traumatic events, has been documented in many armed conflicts including those in Bangladesh, Cambodia, Cyprus, Haiti, Liberia, Somalia and Uganda." "Rape was a weapon of terror as the German Hun marched through Belgium in World War I; gang rape was part of the orchestrated riots of Kristallnacht which marked the beginning of Nazi campaigns against the Jews. It was a weapon of revenge as the Russian Army marched to Berlin in World War II, it was used when the Japanese raped Chinese women in the city of Nanking, when the Pakistani Army battled Bangladesh, and when the American G.I.s made rape in Vietnam a 'standard operating procedure aimed at terrorizing the population into submission."----- Ancient times until World War 2."------

Rape as a weapon of war is seen as one of the great mass crimes of modern times with it adding its own brand of shame to wars. From conflicts in Bosnia to Uganda thousands of women and girls have been victims to this traumatising crime, with many of these rapes leading to victims being murdered or committing suicide.

It's more about the shared assumptions about masculinity and sexuality that makes it such a powerful weapon that soldiers use without necessarily having been given orders.

Dating as far back as the Japanese occupation of Nanking in 1937, rape as a weapon of war has been prevalent in conflicts throughout the 1990s and continues to be used today. A common misconception is that rape is simply a by-product of war. Sexual violence is certainly occurring in every conflict around the world but its role has evolved from an unfortunate effect of war to a tactic used to humiliate and control entire populations.

Rape as weapon of war, is not something new, for ages such heinous crime has been committed against women, in the 1990's when the erstwhile Yugoslavia got disintegrated and the various region of it plunged into bloody civil war, some of the most horrific crimes were committed against women in Bosnia by the Serbian forces, when Sex terror was unleashed on them, it has been reported that many Muslim women were brutally Raped by the Serb forces and to add to the misery of beleaguered women and to their dismay most of these women were allegedly rape in front of their Father, brothers, husband and children.

In Bosnia "Women were raped so they could give birth to a Serbian baby." The same tactic was used in a "very strategic attack" by state-backed Pakistani troops during the fight for Bangladesh's independence in 1971. Whether a woman is raped at gunpoint or trafficked into sexual slavery by an occupying force, the sexual abuse will shape not just her own but her community's future for years to come.

There are testimonies from Bosnian women who had soldiers tell them, while raping them, that they wanted to get them pregnant or force them to have children who would look ethnically different from their mother, or that they were raping them to punish them for being Muslim (or Croatian). There were also women who became pregnant and were forced to carry their babies to term.

Genocidal rape against the **Bosniak** (Bosnian Muslim) ethnic group. Estimates of the total number of women raped during the war range from 12,000 to 50,000. The **International Criminal Tribunal** for the former Yugoslavia (ICTY) declared that "systematic rape", and "sexual enslavement" in time of war was a crime against humanity, second only to the war crime of genocide. Although the ICTY did not treat the mass rapes as genocide, it is clear from the organized, and systematic nature of the mass rapes of the Bosniak female population, that these rapes were a part of a larger campaign of genocide. While women of all ethnic groups were affected by instances of rape during the conflict, the great majority of war crimes were perpetrated by the Bosnian Serb forces and Serb paramilitary units, who used rape as an instrument of terror as part of their programme of ethnic cleansing.

Violence against women, especially rape, has added its own brand of shame to recent wars. From conflicts in Bosnia and Herzegovina to Peru to Rwanda, girls and women have been singled out for rape, imprisonment, torture and execution. Rape, identified by psychologists as the most intrusive of traumatic events, has been documented in many armed conflicts including those in Bangladesh, Cambodia, Cyprus, Haiti, Liberia, Somalia and Uganda.

Systematic rape is often used as a weapon of war in 'ethnic cleansing'. More than 20,000 Muslim girls and women have been raped in Bosnia since fighting began in April 1992, according to a European Community fact-finding team. Teenage girls have been a particular target in Bosnia and Herzegovina and Croatia, according to "The State of the World's Children 1996 report." The report also says that impregnated girls have been forced to bear 'the enemy's' child.

Myanmar's transition to democracy following five decades of brutal military rule has won widespread international praise, but rights' groups say little has changed in resource-rich border areas, where the army continues to grapple with stubborn ethnic insurgencies. As in the past, the use of sexual violence against civilians is widespread and systematic.

"Rights activists in Myanmar, also known as Burma, say the army continues to use rape as a weapon of war nearly three years after President Thein Sein's nominally civilian government ended a half-century of brutal military rule. The Women's League of Burma released a report documenting more than 100 rapes, almost all in townships plagued by stubborn ethnic insurgencies. Nearly half were brutal gang rapes, several of the victims were children, and 28 of the women were killed or died from their injuries, as confirmed by "Tin Tin Nyo, the Women league's general secretary."

Rape and sexual abuse are not just a by-product of war but are used as a deliberate military strategy, it says. The opportunistic rape and pillage of previous centuries has been replaced in modern conflict by rape used as an orchestrated combat tool.

According to RAINN.org, there are approximately 237,868 victims (age 12 or older) of sexual assault each year. Every 2 minutes an American is sexually assaulted... and 1 out of every 6 American women has been the victim of an attempted or completed rape in her lifetime. These are disgusting, but, unfortunate facts.

While the history of wars and conflicts is replete with systematic incidents of sexual violence against vulnerable women, modern-day wars have witnessed large-scale indiscriminate deployment of rape as a "weapon" of war by combatants. In recent armed conflicts — such as in the former Yugoslavia, Liberia, the Democratic Republic of the Congo, Sudan, the Central African Republic, Sierra Leone and Rwanda — the widespread use of rape as a tool of warfare has become a conspicuous phenomenon.

Rape is the most powerful, cost-effective weapon available for destroying the lives of "enemy" women, families, and entire communities, demoralizing enemy forces, and, in some cases, accomplishing genocide. Rape is being used more than any other prohibited weapon of war including starvation, attacks on cultural objects; and the use of herbicides, biological or chemical weapons, dum-dum bullets, white phosphorus or blinding lasers.

Rape has been a dishonourable camp follower of war for as long as armies have marched into battle. In the 20th century, perceptions of rape in war have moved from something that is inevitable when men are deprived of female companionship for prolonged periods to an actual tactic in conflict. The lasting psychological harm that rape inflicts on its victims has also been recognized:

Rape is always torture, says Manfred Nowak, Special Rapporteur on torture and other cruel, inhuman or degrading treatment or punishment.

"Soeren Kern **published an article** about child sex slavery in the UK. He focuses on a report about the large-scale "grooming" of non-Muslim girls age between 11&16 by gangs of Muslim men into sex slavery. These men do not prey upon Muslim girls. The government, police force, and media have been "multi-culturally correct" and very reluctant to expose this phenomenon or to charge these men. Many feminists would say that men all over the world buy and sell women, kidnap or trick them into prostitution. And they are right. But they are wrong to refuse to focus on Paedophelia Sex Slavery wherever and whenever this monster rears its ugly head. The prepared report is meticulous. It documents that "officials in England and Wales were aware of rampant child grooming—the process by which sexual predators befriend and build trust with children in order to prepare them for abuse—by Muslim gangs since at least 1988."

Imagine that. Imagine being a young girl abused and the very people you are told will help you close their doors on you and worse still blames you for the abuse! The young women concerned are often seen by the Police as being deviant or promiscuous. The adult men with whom they are seen with are not questioned.

These accounts give us a harrowing perspective of the scale of the problem. How do we safeguard young vulnerable girls from those who want to exploit them? How do we inform the public to recognise a child who is being groomed? What use is all of this if the authorities are not going to help bring perpetrators to justice?

Not just women, but, Male gender is not spared as well, there are many incidents reported of men being raped and sexually tortured during wars, also when men's are held as prisoner of war; The facts of brutality men experiences during captivity are horrific, with reports of men not just being raped, but systematically raped by large group of men, repeatedly and resolutely, to deliberately maximize the physical and mental damage. Sexual violence against men is used as a weapon of war around the world, not just in Africa but in past conflicts in Bosnia, Iran, Chile... Surveys of political prisoners, from Sarajevo to El Salvador, have reported up to 80 per cent of male prisoners having been raped.

During the wars in Bosnia and Croatia in the early "19' Nineties," male rape and sexual torture were used as a weapon of war with serious consequences for the victims' mental, physical, and sexual health, Balkan experts says.

Despite the fact that hundreds of Bosnian men are believed to be victims of wartime rapes and sexual abuse, only two non-governmental organisations in Bosnia with limited resources provide them with psychological help. Their status has not been properly regulated by law either. "Men were forced to have sexual intercourse in front of other inmates. This, of course, caused them great physical and psychological pain."

According to testimonies of some of Bosnian war crime victims, the victims were sexually assaulted with glass bottles, guns and truncheons. Also, castrations were allegedly performed by crude means - such as forcing other detainees to bite off a prisoner's testicles. The witnesses also said that prisoners had been forced to commit other types of abuse on each other, and several men made statements that fathers and sons had been coerced into performing sexual acts upon each other.

When a crime doesn't exist in the eyes of the law, there's little support, protection or justice. But it's also the shame that stops many men from reporting what happened to them. "It's a taboo in civil society for a man to admit he's been raped. "There's confusion from people about the difference between sexual violence and homosexuality.

It's this stigma that makes male rape such a difficult subject to shine a light on. It's extremely difficult to get people to talk; There are very high levels of shame and a very high fear of stigmatization around people's masculinity, being seen as not a 'real man'. When women get raped, the accusation is that they've become prostitutes. With men, it's that they've become homosexuals or women.

Sexual violence in the Democratic Republic of Congo (DRC) is endemic. Abuses are committed by government forces, including la Police Nationale Congolaise (the PNC), and the rebel groups FARDC and FDLR. Rape often forms part of a larger terror campaign where victims are subjected to looting and torture.

According to preliminary results from the International Men and Gender Equality Survey (IMAGES) **more than one in three Men** surveyed in the Democratic Republic of the Congo's war-torn east **admits committing sexual assault**, and three in four believe that a woman who "does not dress decently is asking to be raped". Impunity for these crimes is the norm, few cases are prosecuted and few perpetrators face justice. However, stigmatization and being ostracized from family members and the community are daily realities for survivors.

Men aren't simply raped, they are forced to penetrate holes in banana trees that run with acidic sap, to sit with their genitals over a fire, to drag rocks tied to their penis, to give oral sex to queues of soldiers, to be penetrated with screwdrivers and sticks. Because there has been so little research into the rape of men during war, it's not possible to say with any certainty why it happens or even how common it is – although a rare 2010 survey, published in the *Journal of the American Medical Association*, found that 22% of men and 30% of women in Eastern Congo reported conflict-related sexual violence.

The research by Lara Stemple at the University of California doesn't only show that male sexual violence is a component of wars all over the world, it also suggests that international aid organisations are failing male victims. Her study cites a review of 4,076 NGOs that have addressed wartime sexual violence. Only 3% of them mentioned the experience of men in their literature. "Typically," Stemple says, "as a passing reference."

That men are victims of sexual assault should not come as news to feminists, especially because it is observed so frequently in prisons, and I also doubt that many feminists deny that women perpetrators of sexual assault against men exist and contribute to the male rape victim demographic. However, the fact that men frequently under-report rape (especially when perpetrated by a woman, but in general), and are less likely to recognize an incident of forcible sex as rape due to stigma, does little to help the cause.

Further, patriarchal attitudes, which are frequently credited with perpetuating female rape culture, are also responsible for the same problems that contribute to the problematic marginalization of male rape. Male-centric ideas, such as that men are stronger than women and cannot be victimized by them, simultaneously cause male privilege in society and male oppression in the context of sexual consent. The harm that these myths do to male victims of sexual assault cannot be overstated, and if men should oppose the patriarchy for no other reason, then at least they ought to consider the harm they do to themselves by perpetuating such ideas. The patriarchy hurts men and women alike, but in very different ways, and the ways in which it hurts men are insidious and subtle.

In twenty-first century the so-called "**Arab Spring revolution**" has proved to become the mother of all human problems ever since the end of 2ⁿᵈ world-war that ended in 1940s.

"**Arab spring**" is the name given by the western media to the Revolutionary Movement, a struggle that started in the year 2011 by the beleaguered and long suppressed Arab citizens to seek civil-rights and better quality of life and freedom of speech, demanding democracy and accountability, the protest demonstrations for freedom from their respective country's <u>ruling dictatorial regimes</u> that first started in a small town of Tunisia soon spread to many west-Asian and North-African Muslim dominated countries. But, what seemingly started in earnest as a sincere peaceful movement to seek democratic rights in which both men and women equally participated to demonstrate against the authoritarian regime in countries like Libya, Egypt, Yemen and Tunisia etc, but, no sooner had the struggle started. The whole concept of revolutionary movement was hijacked by the opportunists Islamists jihadi forces and it was twisted and turned into full blown communal and sectarian conflict, deliberately taking advantage of generation old divide between Shia and Sunni and bitter rivalry amongst various religious and ethnic communities in Islamic world by many alleged state sponsor groups of extremist Islamic fundamentalist forces.

The Salafist belonging to Sunni-Muslim fundamentalist jihadi (holy-warriors) groups turned the Arab spring protest into full fledge sectarian and communal conflict, to achieve their selfish objective the Islamic jihadist groups like the most notorious amongst them "ISIS, Al-Qaeda, Al-Nusra and BOKO Haram," started to terrorise people and cause havoc in the civil society, the monstrous

Islamic elements brutally started enforcing their insular outdated chemistry of extreme hard-core Islamic religious practice on common people.

Particularly hard pressed are/were the women belonging to almost every religious and racial communities. The Islamic militants brazenly intimidate folks belonging to all the Non Sunni Muslim communities, and even the followers of Sunni-Islam especially those people who are liberal and secular are not spared, the Islamists jihadists or to say the 'Muslim terrorists' intimidate even the Sunni-Muslim folks who are secular and liberal and threatens them of dire consequences if they do not follow the strict Islamic sharia law and abide by it, these jihadist groups have not hesitated even in raping and killing Sunni-Muslims those who dare to oppose their diktat.

In the Arab spring conflict the Islamic militants have reserved their harsh brutality for Non-Sunni Muslims, they are fierce and callous when it comes to dealing with civilians belonging to communities such as the Shia's, Christians, Kurdish, Jewish, Yazidi's etc, the various Sunni-Muslim jihadist ostentatiously loots wealth, ferociously rapes women.

A new concept has emerged in the Arab Spring conflict **"SEX – JIHAD"** something unheard of by even the staunch Sunni-Muslim religious leaders as well, when some of the Salafist clerics belonging to Sunni Islam sect, made appeal to young Sunni Muslim women and girls to participate in jihad in a unique way and to play a role in establishing the Islamic caliphate in Iraq, Syria, Jordan and Lebanon, the appeal to the girls and women of Muslim community was to participate in jihad by surrendering their bodies to appease and to soothe the minds of the voracious jihadists by sleeping with them.

The most fearful extremist group **ISIS** (Islamic state of Iraq & Al-sham) owing allegiance to "Sunni–Islam" has been wreaking havoc across the Middle-East Arabian countries in what is largely communal conflict between two prominent Islamic denomination (Shia and Sunni), with waging war showing no sign of abating, Their (ISISI) latest savage demand is sure to send shock-wave throughout the civilized world – **"hand us over your young daughters/widows for sex jihad, or else."**

The Islamic Supreme Council of America defines a fatwa as an "Islamic legal pronouncement, issued by an expert in religious law (mufti)," pertaining to a specific issue, usually at the request of an individual or judge to resolve an issue where Islamic jurisprudence (fiqh), is unclear." Thus, the radicals in the ISIS organization have taken the pronouncement permitting Jihad al-Nikah (jihad of legal copulation) very seriously.

The militant Islamist group ISIS (the Islamic State in Iraq and Syria) put up posters calling on the people of Mosul to bring forward for them their unmarried girls to participate in "*Jihad al-Nikah*," or sex jihad. The reports came from Al-Masryalyoum, a well-respected Egyptian daily newspaper as well as other sources in the Arab press.

ISIS after gaining control over vast territories in northern Iraq including Mosul, Iraq's second largest city. *Jihad al-Nikah* refers to women joining the jihad by offering sex to the male fighters.

Posters in public places in Mosul read:

"We call upon the people of this county to bring their unmarried girls so they can fulfil their duty in sex jihad for their warrior brothers in the city and anyone who will not appear will feel the full force of the *sharia* [Islamic law] upon him/her."

ISIS fighters are ordering terrified families in Iraq to hand over their daughters for sex. Leaflets in the captured cities of Mosul and Tikrit claim the women – virgins or not – must join Jihad, or Holy war, and cleanse themselves by sleeping with jihadi "(from non-Muslim perspective the jihadists are **terrorists**, but from Islam perspective the *jihadists* are **sacred** and Muslim folks considers jihadists as saviour of their faith hence are holy and admirable)."

The consequences of refusal to submit to sex jihad are beatings or death. The Jihad al-Nikah often incorporates beatings and transference to many different men for all sorts of sexual acts. Leaflets distributed in the Iraqi cities tell families that they must hand over their daughters for sex jihad, and that "those that refuse to do so are violating God's will."

Jihad al-Nikah, (Jihad al-Nikah is an Arabic phrase meaning "sexual holy war,") permitting extramarital sexual relations with multiple partners, is considered by some hard-line Sunni Muslim Salafists as a legitimate form of holy war.

Reports emanated from Mosul indicated that ISIS fighters resorted to going door-to-door, entering houses, killing the men and raping the women. Al-Iraqiya TV station published a report about the story of two Iraqi girls who were raped by the armed men of ISIS in Mosul. The two girls, who are sisters, reportedly said that ISIS fighters came into their house, killed the male members of the family and afterwards, they took it in turns of raping the women.

So, Technically known as a Jihad al-Nika'h (often translated as Sexual Holy War or Holy War of Prostitution), highly renown Saudi cleric Sheikh Mohamad bin Abdul Rahman al-Arefe, Chief Imam of the Mosque of the King Fahd Academy of the Royal Saudi Navy issued a fatwa (Islamic theological ruling) authorizing girls as young as 14 to step forward to make sacrifices in the name of Islamic Jihad. Among the sacrifices expected of the women and girls was they surrender "their chastity" as well as "their dignity" as reported by the Assyrian International News Service on June 24, 2013. Considering Jihad al-Nika'h as a legitimate form of holy war, Sunni-Muslim women and girls from Britain, Iraq, Malaysia and Australia have reportedly volunteered to offer themselves in "temporary marriages," usually lasting only as long as it take for an ISIS jihadists to sexually gratify themselves.

Many young girls and women from countries such as Somalia, Tunisia, Egypt as well from prosperous European countries like Britain, France and Netherlands, heeded to the call given by the Islamic clerics and willingly surrendered their body for what these girls perceived as mandatory holy duty, and travelled to countries like Syria and Iraq and slept or still are serving their body to the cunning jihadi men.

Records have also proved that Australian, British, and Malaysian Sunni Muslim women travelled to Iraq and Syria to participate in Jihad al-Nikah, or sexual jihad, and willingly joined Islamic State (ISIS) terrorists. They intended to becoming comfort women for the jihadists as the Sunni men continue to fight explosive wars to establish Caliphate in Iraq and Syria. "These women are believed to have offered themselves in sexual comfort roles to ISIS fighters who are attempting to establish Islamic rule in the Mid-east," said one source in Malaysia, further adding, "This concept may seem controversial but it has arisen because certain Muslim women here (Malaysia) are showing sympathy for the ISIS struggle." "Checks with our foreign counterparts and intelligence disseminated reveal that there may be up to 50 Malaysians women in the Middle East."

Over 600 British Muslims are believed to be fighting for "ISIS" in the conflict in Syria and Iraq. The number also includes "British Muslim women who are not fighting on the front line, but are still involved by performing sexual jihad", confirms the intelligence official.

In Britain and the Netherlands, where Muslim gangs have been involved in targeting teenage girls for sex, drugs, gang-rape and child sex slavery 'Love Jihad' transforms into 'Sex Jihad'. Vulnerable Sikh girls were apparently targets of Muslim gangs in the 1980s, and White teenagers in the last 15 years. The scandal never came to light due to the political correctness of the British police force and the media, which found it difficult to name the culprits for fear of being accused of racism. But apart from political correctness, virulent patriarchy is the villain in 'Sex Jihad', too. Women are the only victims here.
'Love Jihad' and 'Sex Jihad' are thus tussles between two or more patriarchies.-

Most of these young Sunni Muslim girls who offered their bodies to be consumed by the terrorist, it has been reported that many of these girls and women apart from unwanted pregnancy they have contracted several Sex related ailments some are believed to have even contracted **Aids** "(HIV)."

The high risk of infection with sexually transmitted diseases (STDs), including HIV/AIDS, accompanies either to those girls who voluntarily surrender their bodies for Sex – Jihad or all other types of sexual violence against women and girls. The movement of refugees and marauding military units and the breakdown of health services and public education worsens the impact of diseases and chances for treatment. For example, one study has suggested that the exchange of sex for protection during the civil war in Uganda in the 1980s was a contributing factor to the country's high rate of AIDS.

One striking difference between the use of rape as a weapon of war in pre-1990 conflicts and in latter-day wars is the emergence and "wilful" transmission of HIV to the victims. Serious questions have been raised in the social science literature about the actual time of transmission and infection, and whether the "intent" of the perpetrators could conclusively be to infect the victim with HIV. Nonetheless, there is evidence from the victims' accounts confirming the deliberate nature of these acts.

One bizarre narrative of an alleged incident that has been reported from Kenya (the identity of the victim and that of the allege perpetrator has been concealed by the authorities for obvious reason), wherein a young Kenyan woman was brutally raped by a man, the young woman a student had allegedly gone to a club to attend a party, the girl had enjoyed a couple of drinks during the party, when she returned back to her hostel room under influence of alcohol, taking advantage of the woman state of mind a cruel man wandering around prying for vulnerable victim spotted this young woman and allegedly followed her attacked her and not only raped that young woman to satisfy his sex desire but he outrageously and deliberately infected the young woman whom he raped with "HIV," then, as a consequence of being raped, what the victim of rape the frustrated young woman did could be termed as equally inhuman, the young girl infected with HIV, she decided to seek revenge for her lost dignity and chastity with entire male gender. To seek revenge, She started luring men and indulged with men craving for fantasy, she sleeping for sex with as many men (its reported, 300+) as possibly she could and its alleged that she had unprotected sex, therefore most men with whom the young beleaguered woman slept with and had sex with, those unfortunate men "have or may potentially have" got infected with HIV' Aids.

Now, what the young woman did to seek revenge for being raped and infected with HIV, it raises one pressing question, what do the scholars and intellectuals would have to say, about the action of beleaguered woman? Is it OK? If someone Mess up your life. You Mess up others life. Is it a fair thing to do? Is it morally and ethically correct to ruin other innocent lives because someone else has destroyed your life? **No, Never**, at least I firmly believe, under duress or frustration don't mess up and please don't destroy others life. "What do you-all think?"

Women who are victims of rape during conflicts have an inalienable right to reparation, psychological and physical rehabilitation, needs access to social measures, and health security. In efforts to reconstruct post-conflict societies, the disarmament, demobilization and reintegration (DDR) processes should include sustainable policies and programmes aimed at holistic reparation for victims of rape during wars and conflicts.

Like other forms of sexual assault, responding to sexual terrorism requires criminal justice, medical, psychological and social initiatives. However, in many cases the girls or women are too scared to come forward for treatment, which hinders efforts to tackle the problem. Despite this, some progress has been made.

Some call it 'rape jihad', others opt for 'sexual terrorism' or 'forced marriage'. Whatever one may choose to call it, when terrorism meets sexual violence it is two crimes too many. It is the use of sexual abuse to spread terror with the intention of controlling or manipulating the government or parts of a population. By intimidating and humiliating families, terrorists hope to exert influence over their targeted audience.

Sexual terrorism is often classified as being gendered in nature, due to the fact that the victims are chiefly girls or women. In sexual terrorism, the rape or assault is part of a broader objective: to spread terror or send a message, a motivation similar to that found in the use of suicide bombings. The perpetrators justify sexual terrorism by claiming that the Prophet Mohammed sanctioned the rape of both non-Muslims (infidels or *kafirs*) and Muslims who do not adhere strictly to Islam.

In August 2013, a young mother in Somalia was kidnapped and raped by members of the terrorist network Al-Shabaab for being a Christian. The terrorists contacted the victim's husband, warning him to convert to Islam. Human Rights Watch has released similar reports on a spate of child kidnappings in Somalia. The kidnapped children were trained to fight and used to protect the adult terrorists. According to the reports, the girls were forced to marry these 'soldiers' or face beheading, after which their heads would be sent back to their schools as a warning against insolence.

In one of the many notorious incident of Sex – Jihad, a 16 year old Syrian girl by the name of "Rawan Milad Al-dah" was rescued from sexual slavery by the Syrian soldiers loyal to its president Assad, the hard-pressed girl "Rawan" took courage to share her ordeal with a TV broadcaster. She was brave enough to keep her face straight while talking about her being sold to the "Rebel free Syrian army terrorist" by her own father as a sex slave in the name of jihad, but do I doubt that the jihadist would use rape as weapon of war in the conflict stricken country like Syria? Not one bit.

It's not unusual for rape to be used as a weapon of war, but this is one of the first indications of the extent it has been used in Libya, since **staggeringly beautiful young woman "Miss Iman al-Obedi"** burst into the hotel housing the foreign journalists in Tripoli in March 2011 and she accused pro-Gaddafi militiamen of gang-raping her. In Libya rape was extensively and profoundly used by the soldiers loyal to Libyan dictator Muammar Gaddafi, there are stories of sex materials like Viagra and condoms being found from the dead bodies of Gaddafi's soldiers. Unprecedented numbers of sex crimes were committed by forces loyal to Gaddafi, women and young girls and boys as well were ferociously raped in Libya.

In Egypt as well the story is no different, instead in the land of pharaohs, its sexual harassment record against women and girls particularly is worse as compare to many other Arab countries. It has been reported that many women and girls participating in pro-democracy movement to gain better civil rights for themselves, but, their participation in most of the pro-democracy (between 2011-2013) protest turned into unforgiving nightmares, horror struck when miscreant men mobbed up and molested and sexually harassed many Egyptian women and girls, the unruly mob didn't stopped at just molesting, but they even went step further at Cairo's famous Tahrir square raped few women in full public view, not just that Egyptian women and girls suffered the menace but few of the foreign journalist travelling to Egypt on assignment to report and cover events of political turmoil in Egypt were not spare either, at least three foreign journalist on separate occasion were either rape or brutally molested by mob of cruel men, these female journalist were doing their duty of reporting unravelling political events.

On the first anniversary of the election of President Mohamed Morsi on June 30-2013, thousands of Egyptians took to the streets in Tahrir Square in Cairo demanding the resignation of Mr Morsi. During the four days of protests, at least 91 women were attacked and sexually assaulted by mobs, while government leaders and police stood by and failed to intervene. Some women required extensive medical surgery after being subjected to brutal gang rapes and sexual assault with sharp objects. After the protests, survivors came forward to tell their horrific stories and demanded better security protection for women. While the protests led to the end of Morsi's presidency, the government downplayed the violence, prompting international calls to improve law enforcement and bring perpetrators to justice. These actions proved fruitless, as security forces again came under fire in August for using live ammunition against citizens resulting in 638 deaths.

Egypt's neighbouring countries in Africa are equally hit by Islamic fundamentalist ideology, one of the biggest country in Africa both economically and in population **Nigeria** is suffering excruciating pain of Islamic extremism, Nigeria based hard-line barbaric Sunni-Muslim terrorist group "Boko Haram" has been attacking civilians and local authorities with increasing vigour. The killings, torture, rape, other forms of sexual violence and abductions, crimes perpetrated by this criminal group against civilians have forced thousands of Nigerians to flee across the borders to seek refuge in neighbouring countries.

Similar to the Taliban in Afghanistan and Pakistan, and the Al-Shabaab group in Somalia, Boko Haram preaches radical Islam, it makes young girls its prime target. Its members pillage and burn schools to the ground, abducts female pupils, to "save them from sin", sells them as slaves, force them into marriage and treat them as trophies of war. Their criminal and misogynous policy aims to deprive women of their basic rights to life, security and education. These atrocities takes place within a context of widespread human rights violations in the Northern parts of Nigeria.

Terrorism in Nigeria, though it is a recent phenomenon, is assuming a dangerous trend with the Islamist terrorist group Boko Haram sect targeting children especially girls and women as weapons for their agitations. In February 2014, over 49 young boys in their boarding school were brutally murdered in a gruesome attack at night in Yobe State, North Eastern part of Nigeria. A few months' earlier, 27 girls and women were abducted by the Boko Haram.

In April 2014, about 270 school girls were abducted in Chibok Borno State in Nigeria and are reported to be sold into sexual slavery by the Boko Haram sect. Since the horrific incident, Boko Haram has periodically abducted more girls and women and killed defenceless boys and men under the pretext of propagating Islamic Religion and opposition to western style of education.

In most part of the world's Socially Conservative society homosexuality is considered as Sin, many of the prominent religions as well do not accept homosexuality. Hence, Gay and lesbian men and women particularly in Muslim dominated countries are distinctly most susceptible to brutal sexual violence. Gay men's have to constantly listen abuses and taunts and are consistently humiliated and raped. Gay men in Muslim countries find themselves untenable hence suffers severe discrimination. A men who is gay and is serving a jail sentence in countries like Pakistan, Syria or Egypt or even Uganda for instance is most certainly likely to be raped and physically abused by other serving inmates as well more likely by the police itself. Many gays and lesbian men and women from countries like Turkey, Lebanon or Egypt escapes from their country and migrates to more socially progressive countries for example "Germany or Sweden" in search for safe harbour, but most of these unfortunates gays and lesbians do not often find peace even in the socially progressive western countries as well, they have to suffer many peculiar types of harassment and sexual exploitation.

The prison cells of developed and socially progressive countries either are not safe for gays, lesbians or transgender, even in USA and European prisons the gay men are sexually discriminated. In prison rape, the perpetrator and victim are almost always the same sex (due to the gender-segregated nature of prison confinement). As such, a host of issues regarding sexual orientation and gender roles are associated with the topic. In U.S. male prisons, rapists generally identify themselves as heterosexual and confine themselves to non-receptive sexual acts. Victims, commonly referred to as "punks" or "bitches", may or may not be seen as homosexual. "Punks" is a term for those who are generally confined to performing receptive sexual acts. Moreover, though "punks" are coerced into a sexual arrangement with an aggressor in exchange for protection, these men generally consider themselves heterosexual.

According to Algerian militant Abu Bacir El Assimi, Islamic terrorists rape young men as a means of recruitment for suicide bombings. Rape creates a social stigma and fear, according to reports, that leave Muslims prepared to die. "The sexual act on young recruits aged between 16 to 19 was a means to urge them to commit suicide operations."

Both rape and homosexual acts under Sharia law are punishable by death.

In one of the news report according News sources say an autopsy revealed a suspected terrorist bomber killed during an attempted terrorist attack on a security installation in Algeria may have been raped. The report presents the autopsy as finding: "a large tear in the anus of the terrorist, which confirms the sexual abuse." The victim of the alleged abuse was 22 years old who was said to have joined a terrorist group in March 2008.

If reports are true about sexual coercion of males or male rape being used to recruit young men to die in acts of terrorism, the concerns about how men are treated after male rape indicates the level of shame and indignities suffered. It was reported in Dubai in 2007 a very young French boy, Alex, age 15, who was kidnapped and sexually assaulted.

Sexual exploitation in corridor of power; Talking about political hierarchy: The notorious kingpins who inflict their dubious "leadership" on nations are often ineffective and arbitrary at best or genocidal at worst. However, the personal lives, beliefs, and happenings behind the scenes as far as dictators are concerned are often simply weird, or defy popular imagination. The odious methods they vehemently use to suppress dissent.

Muammar Gaddafi could well be described as Sex Terrorist, "BBC documentary has eyewitness accounts of murder, torture and sexual abuse by the Libyan dictator, who was shot by rebels in 2011. Ousted Libyan dictator Muammar Gaddafi kidnapped and raped hundreds of teenagers in specially built sex dungeons, according to a **television documentary that was screened by BBC. The program titled, "Storyville: Mad Dog – Gaddafi's Secret World,"** Victims and witnesses state in the documentary that Gaddafi would choose his targets on visits to schools or colleges, patting on the head those who caught his eye.

Gaddafi security officials would then take the victim to one of several specially designed suites of rooms, where they would be abused and raped by the dictator. In one such suite at Tripoli University, there was found to be a fully-equipped gynaecological examination room, where victims were tested for sexually transmitted diseases before being sexually abused.

"Some of the girls were only 14 years old," recalled one teacher at a Tripoli school. "They would simply take the girl they wanted. They had no conscience, no morals, not an iota of mercy, even though she was a mere child." Some of the girls were held for years, while others were dumped with appalling injuries. Some victims were drafted into Gaddafi's unit of private female bodyguards, enduring years of rape and abuse and forced to witness the execution of opponents to the regime.

"The women would first be raped by the dictator then passed on, like used objects, to one of his sons and eventually to high-ranking officials for more sexual abuse," said Benghazi-based psychologist Seham Sergewa, who interviewed victims for the International Criminal Court.

Boys were also forced to serve in Gaddafi's harem. "He was terribly sexually deviant," recalled former chief of protocol Nuri Al Mismari. "Young boys and so on. He had his own boys. They used to be called the 'services group'."……

Once Gaddafi invited 20 young Italian models on a two-week all-expenses paid trip to Libya. A junket, if you will. The models (and by models, I mean prostitutes) later said that Gaddafi treated them like queens, but all denied the existence of the actual sex parties. (Or "bunga bunga" parties, in the parlance of our times).

Monstrous former Libyan dictator Gaddafi's death was as horrendous same as much the horror he committed in his life time. He was dragged from a drainpipe and shot by rebels in 2011, during Libya's civil war.

Former Iraqi dictator Saddam Hussein had two bloodthirsty sons who were just as crazy as he was – Uday and Qusay. Out of the entire terrible trio, Uday is thought to be the worst, an unforgiving psychopath who delighted only in sadism and cruelty. Until the US-led invasion of Iraq in 2003, little was known about the day-to-day lives of Uday and Qusay Hussein. But once Iraqis began to talk to the media, a seemingly never-ending string of unimaginably grim, grotesque stories began to emerge.

Most infamous is the account (recreated in the film *The Devil's Double*, about Uday and one of his personal decoys) concerns a 14-year-old girl – the daughter of a former provincial governor – with whom Uday became infatuated after spotting her at a party. Uday's bodyguards at first tried to simply lure her up to meet with the boss man, but she refused. When she reappeared three days later, she had been raped, but also provided with a new dress, a new watch, and some money. Her father complained to Saddam, and then went public with the story, leading Uday to threaten to kill the governor unless he submitted both of his daughters (the other one was 12 at that time) to be his new 'girlfriends.' The governor complied.

But that's just one story. There are other anecdotes, many of them almost too hideous to recount. One story tells of Uday crashing a wedding and kidnapping and raping the bride, leading the groom to kill himself. Another bride was raped and burned with chemicals while still in her wedding dress. Uday reportedly was so jealous of his brother Qusay (thought to be Saddam's favoured son), he insisted that any women who slept with his brother had to be kidnapped and brought to him for rape and torture. Sometimes he would utilize bizarre or historical methods of torture that he found out about on the Internet. Use of an iron maiden was said to be among his favourites. Uday's less violent but still peculiar proclivities over the long years of his father's absolute rule also captured the world's attention in 2003. Five nights a week, he'd throw private parties at the posh Baghdad Boat Club, with a rotating crop of beautiful young women invited for drinking and dancing. Near the close of the party, the female guests would be lined up and Uday would choose his favourites to keep for the night. He apparently never slept with the same girl more than two or three times. (The parties were only five nights a week, as Uday took two nights a week off from girls. "Fasting," as he called it.)

An ill man who had been grievously injured in an attempt on his life in 1996, Uday tried all sorts of unconventional remedies to cure himself, including bringing in a new mother to breastfeed him. (He hoped that the vitamin-rich milk might help to cure him. Plus I think he probably just enjoyed it too.)

Sex terror is not something new, discrimination against women is as old as recorded history, despite several feminist movement the world over demanding more equal rights for women and gender equality, these feminist movement have not succeeded in achieving their objectives.

Patriarchal religions, which mould most of the cultures of the world, subordinate women and girls to men. Fundamentalist movements, whether Christian, Jewish, Hindu or Islamic, advocate the repression of women and girls' sexuality. Women and girls' interaction with men and boys is closely monitored and restricted and their bodies and hair covered in a way deemed to be modest. For example, under the influence of Islamic fundamentalism, women are required to wear full body coverings, such as chadors and burqas. Punishment for sexual misconduct can be severe, as in Iran, where women can be legally stoned to death. The other form of control and abuse of women's sexuality is exploitation, in which women and girls are used for men's sexual gratification or profit. Women and children are sexually exploited when they are subjected to incest, rape, sexual harassment, battering, bride trafficking, pornography, and prostitution.

The law should delineate and prohibit behaviour which is socially abhorrent, against odious character. Of course, forcing women to have sex is much easier when the ladies are not highly trained Killing machines. The women are typically characterized as prophets of doom.

Women and women rights groups constant laments about inequality, discrimination in getting jobs and promotions and of sexual harassment at home or at workplace on beaches and in parks.

Domination by men of women is found in the Ancient near East as far back as 3100 BCE, as are restrictions on a woman's reproductive capacity and exclusion from "the process of representing or the construction of history." With the appearance of the Hebrews, there is also "the exclusion of woman from the God-humanity covenant."

Famine, starvation and mass-migrations related to land-abandonment severely traumatised the originally peaceful and sex-positive inhabitants of those lands, inducing a distinct turning away from original Matrism towards patristic forms of behaviour. In medieval Europe, patriarchy was not absolute, as female Empresses (such as **Theodora**) and Matriarchs (such as Helena, the mother of **Constantine**) enjoyed privilege, political rule, and societal honour.

Chapter 2

The strategic use of rape in war is not a new phenomenon but only recently has it begun to be documented, chiefly in the Democratic Republic of Congo, Colombia and Sudan.

Sexual violation of women erodes the fabric of a community in a way that few weapons can. Rape's damage can be devastating because of the strong communal reaction to the violation and pain stamped on entire families. The harm inflicted in such cases on a woman by a rapist is an attack on her family and culture, as in many societies women are viewed as repositories of a community's cultural and spiritual values.

In modern history, rape was used in World War II by the Nazi's, Soviets, and by the Japanese (as was the case with 'Comfort Women' and the infamous Rape of Nanking), and it was also used in Vietnam. The last decade has seen a growing number of civil conflicts around the world that directly target women and girls. The numbers of rapes and other forms of sexual abuse have reached alarming levels, thus constituting an epidemic of sexual violence as a form of warfare. Countries such as: Afghanistan, Bangladesh, Guatemala, India, Liberia, Pakistan, Sierra Leone, Uganda, Sudan and the Congo, to name only a few have used, or currently use, rape as a weapon in conflict. In both a modern and historical context it is clear that all armies use rape as a weapon.

From the systematic rape of women in Bosnia, to an estimated 200,000 women raped during the battle for Bangladeshi independence in 1971, to Japanese rapes during the 1937 occupation of Nanking - the past century offers too many examples. So what motivates armed forces, whether state-backed troops or irregular militia, to attack civilian women and children? Rape is often used in ethnic conflicts as a way for attackers to perpetuate their social control and redraw ethnic boundaries, "Women are seen as the reproducers and carers of the community." "Therefore if one group wants to control another they often do it by impregnating women of the other community because they see it as a way of destroying the opposing community."

Germany in the spring of 1945. Hitler's Nazi regime was on the brink of defeat in the catastrophic war it had launched six years earlier. After invading and occupying large swathes of Eastern Europe and the Soviet Union -- and murdering tens of millions of people in the process -- the German army was retreating, and the Red Army was following hot on its heels, intent on revenge.

One of the twentieth century's greatest crimes, and probably one of the greatest crimes against women in history, was the mass rape of the conquered women of Europe after the Judeo-Communist victory there in 1945. The rapists were mainly Soviet Union (Russian) Red Army soldiers, some of them non-White troops from the Far East and Central Asian Republics of the Soviet Union. They were brutes no doubt, but they were permitted and encouraged to indulge their lower than bestial urges by official "Allied" policies which incited hatred particularly against the Germans, but also against those of other European nationalities which were then allied with Germany in an anti-Communist bloc. One cannot contemplate this great mass orgy of rape, gang rape, and sexual slavery of innocent women and little girls without revulsion.

Sweeping across German territory, many of the Russian soldiers burned, killed, looted. And they also raped German women. The Soviets, of course, weren't the only ones, soldiers from other Allied armies were also guilty of sexual violence as they moved into Germany from the West. But most agree that the problem was particularly acute in eastern Germany. Historians estimate that close to 2 million German women and girls were raped in the closing months of the war, many women were repeatedly raped.

As the Red Army advanced towards her in 1945, the German city of Berlin had become a city virtually without men. Out of a civilian population of 2,700,000, 2,000,000 were women. It is small wonder that the fear of sexual attack raced through the city like a plague. Doctors were besieged by patients seeking information on the quickest way to commit suicide, and poison was in great demand. This ghastly crime perpetrated mainly by what US President Franklin Roosevelt called "our noble Soviet ally."

A wave of rapes and sexual violence occurred in Central Europe in 1944–45, as the Western Allies and the Red Army fought their way into the Third Reich. On the territory of the Nazi Germany, it began on 21 October 1944 when troops of the Red Army crossed the bridge over the Angerapp creek (marking the border) and committed the **Nemmersdorf massacre** before they were beaten back a few hours later.

The majority of the assaults were committed in the Soviet occupation zone, estimates of the numbers of German women raped by Soviet soldiers ranged up to 2 million. In many cases women were the victims of repeated rapes, some as many as 60 to 70 times. At least 100,000 women are believed to have been raped in **Berlin**, based on surging abortion rates in the following months and contemporary hospital reports, with an estimated 10,000 women dying in the aftermath. Female deaths in connection with the rapes in Germany, overall, are estimated at 240,000. **Antony Beevor** describes it as the "greatest phenomenon of mass **rape** in history", and has concluded that at least 1.4 million women were raped in East Prussia, Pomerania and Silesia alone.

Asian men of Mongolian origins and Central Asians were brought to Berlin including Black soldiers from U.S and France. Black soldiers from America and France over 10,000 in Germany and Berlin, some thousands of German white women were raped. There were hundreds to thousands of abandoned brown babies born from Black soldiers of African origin in Germany. Mongolian and Central Asian troops mostly in Berlin. Some German historians claim that 100,000 German white women rape were committed by Asian men of mostly Mongolian origin and including central Asian origin (Kazakh, Kyrgyz) many of those rape victim the white German women were hospitalized, killed or committed suicide.

Historian Norman Naimark writes that after the summer of 1945, Soviet soldiers caught raping civilians were usually punished to some degree, ranging from arrest to execution. However, the rapes continued until the winter of 1947–48, when Soviet occupation authorities finally confined Soviet troops to strictly guarded posts and camps, separating them from the residential population in the Soviet zone of Germany.

In December of 1937, the Japanese Imperial Army marched into China's capital city of Nanking and proceeded to murder 300,000 out of 600,000 civilians and soldiers in the city. The six weeks of carnage would become known as the Rape of Nanking and represented the single worst atrocity during the World War II era in either the European or Pacific Theatres of War.

The elimination of the Chinese POWs began after they were transported by trucks to remote locations on the outskirts of Nanking. As soon as they were assembled, the savagery began, with young Japanese soldiers encouraged by their superiors to inflict maximum pain and suffering upon individual POWs as a way of toughening themselves up for future battles, and also to eradicate any civilized notions of mercy. Filmed footage and still photographs taken by the Japanese themselves document the brutality. Smiling soldiers can be seen conducting bayonet practice on live prisoners, decapitating them and displaying severed heads as souvenirs, and proudly standing among mutilated corpses. Some of the Chinese POWs were simply mowed down by machine-gun fire while others were tied-up, soaked with gasoline and burned alive.

After the destruction of the POWs, the soldiers turned their attention to the women of Nanking and an outright animalistic hunt ensued. Old women over the age of 70 as well as little girls under the age of 8 were dragged off to be sexually abused. More than 20,000 females (with some estimates as high as 80,000) were gang-raped by Japanese soldiers, then stabbed to death with bayonets or shot so they could never bear witness. Pregnant women were not spared. In several instances, they were raped, then had their bellies slit open and the foetuses torn out. Sometimes, after storming into a house and encountering a whole family, the Japanese forced Chinese men to rape their own daughters, sons to rape their mothers, and brothers their sisters, while the rest of the family was made to watch.

The phrase "comfort women" is a controversial term that refers to approximately 200,000 women who were recruited as prostitutes by the Imperial Japanese Army during World War II. Many of the young women were forced into servitude and exploited as sex slaves throughout Asia, becoming victims of the largest case of human trafficking in the 20th century. The trade of comfort women is thus a massive violation of human rights that's been left out of our textbooks, leaving the individuals embroiled in the atrocious practice to be remembered merely as abstract characters in a taboo history.

'Comfort woman' is a translation of the Japanese euphemism, Jugun Janfu, The first comfort station was established in the Japanese concession in Shanghai in 1932. Earlier comfort women were Japanese prostitutes who volunteered for such service. However, as Japan continued military expansion, the military found itself short of Japanese volunteers, and turned to the local population to coerce women into serving in these stations. Many women responded to calls for work as factory workers or nurses, and did not know that they were being pressed into sexual slavery. The military turned to acquiring comfort women outside mainland Japan, especially from Korea and occupied China. Many women were tricked or defrauded into joining the military brothel. When the locals, especially Chinese, were considered hostile, Japanese soldiers carried out the "Three All's Policy" which included indiscriminately kidnapping and raping local civilians.

In Europe, **German military brothels** were set up by the Third Reich (**Nazi Germany** and the **Third Reich** are common names for Germans during the period from 1933 to 1945, when its government was controlled by Adolf Hitler and his National Socialist German Workers' Party (NSDAP), commonly known as the Nazi Party) during World-war 2 throughout much of occupied Europe for the use of **Wehrmacht** and Schutz-Staffel soldiers. These brothels were generally new creations but in the West they were sometimes set up using existing brothels. Until 1942, there were around 500 military brothels of this kind in Nazi occupied Europe. Often operating in confiscated hotels and guarded by the **Wehrmacht**, these facilities used to serve travelling soldiers and those withdrawn from the front. It is estimated that, along with those in **concentration camp brothels**, at least 34,140 European women were forced to serve as prostitutes during the German occupation. In many cases in Eastern Europe, the women involved were kidnapped on the streets of occupied cities during German military and police round ups.

In an attempt to shine light on this oft-forgotten segment of WWII history," "Most were teenagers... and were raped by between 10 to 100 soldiers a day at military rape camps," "Women were starved, beaten, tortured, and killed. By some estimates only 25 to 30 percent survived the ordeal." Human trafficking is the fastest growing industry in the world, and the second largest business after arms dealing in the 21st century. So, the comfort women issue is not just about the past, but it is very relevant even today.

I want y'all to imagine an orgy of rape like this happening in your country, in your neighbourhood, to your family, to your wife, your sister, your daughter. I want you to imagine what it would feel like to be totally powerless to stop it from happening, completely unable to bring the criminals to justice.

Journalists and human rights organization have documented campaigns of genocidal rape during the conflicts in the Balkans, **Sierra-Leone**, Rwanda, Liberia, Sudan, Uganda, and the **Democratic Republic of Congo**. The strategic aim of these mass rapes are twofold. The first is to instil terror in the civilian population, with the intent to forcibly dislocate them from their property. The second is to degrade the chance of possible return and reconstitution by inflicting humiliation and shame on the targeted population. These effects are strategically important for non-state actors, as it is necessary for them to remove the targeted population from the land. The use of mass rape is well suited for campaigns which involve ethnic cleansing and genocide, as the objective is to destroy or forcefully remove the target population, and ensure they do not return.

It is estimated that nearly six million people have died in the **Democratic Republic of Congo** since 1996 as a result of conflict and conflict related causes (as much as 90% due to malaria, diarrhea, pneumonia and malnutrition, aggravated by displaced population living in unsanitary and over-crowded conditioned that lacked access to shelter, water, food and medicine), nearly 50 percent of them children under the age of Five. Forty-five thousand continue to die each month.

Hundreds of thousands of women have been raped as a weapon of war. One study estimates that as many as 400,000 women may be raped there each year. Additionally, sexual assault is visited on men and children at an incomprehensible level, all of which serves to destabilize, divide and destroy the spirit of the people.

In some raids in Rwanda, virtually every adolescent girl who survived an attack by the militia was subsequently raped. Many of those who became pregnant were ostracized by their families and communities. Some abandoned their babies, while others committed suicide.

War and civil unrest also contribute to increase violence in the home, according to recent studies. Death, upheaval and poverty increase tensions within the family and the likelihood of violence against girls and women. Men who feel that they have lost the ability to protect their women may compensate by exercising violent control over them at home.

The beginning of the end of the use of rape as a weapon of war is to combat gender inequalities and stereotypes in cultures while in peace time, as a method to prevent and curb the use of rape as a weapon of war. Removing the stigma of rape is the first and foremost crucial step to see that the ripple effects do not continue to haunt our global society in future generations and centuries.

Representatives of the 200,000 "comfort women" forcibly drafted into military sexual slavery by Japan from 1928 until the end of World War II are still fighting for restitution. Far from colluding, women from Korea, China, Taiwan, the Philippines, Malaysia and East Timor were "severely coerced" into prostitution.

The tolerance and standardization of rape as a weapon of war is what has led to its impunity at an international scale, and thus increased its silence. Impunity regarding the increasingly brutalization of the use of rape as a weapon of war, combined with its effectiveness, only provokes its use. The reason for such is that the perpetrators are less likely to be tried and punished for the use of this weapon during times of armed conflict than any other weapon, and if convictions do follow the punishment is disproportionate to the crime.

With the world waking up to how serious the issue of rape is, governments need to ensure severe sanctions are in place to ensure that rape is not used as a weapon of war. It is time to punish states that use rape as an unlawful weapon in armed conflict.

The failure to treat war rape like other illegal weapons or war tactics removes the central protection of the laws governing the conduct of war from rape victims, mainly women and girls. Victims' rights to accountability and reparations for their injuries from the use of illegal weapons is separate and in addition to their rights to accountability for other crimes arising out of the same act, including having perpetrators charged with rape as a war crime, a crime against humanity or a constituent element of genocide.

The emergence of HIV/AIDS in the past two decades, and the complex interaction between the virus and conflicts, has reinforced both the human and state security dimensions of disease. Whilst the state security dimension focuses on the collapse of the apparatus of governance, the human security dimension focuses on threats to the vulnerable groups, especially women and girls, during conflicts.

Although the history of wars and conflicts is replete with massive and systematic sexual violence against vulnerable women, modern-day wars in African nations and elsewhere are increasingly characterized by the use of rape as a weapon of war, the intentional or wilful transmission of the HIV to innocent victims, and the neglect of these victims in post-conflict reconstruction programmes. The magnitude of sexual violence in conflict situations will never be fully known, since the stigma associated with being a victim discourages women and girls from reporting the crime.

There is no doubt that the effects of the use of rape as a weapon of war are effects far-reaching regardless of time, place or culture. Short and long-term support and treatment for victims is substantially lacking, which will only serve to exacerbate the use of rape as weapon of war. Thus an end to the perception that rape is a common and unavoidable tactic of war must occur, making it unequivocally unacceptable. In order to do this there are three main areas of focus which must be in place:

1) One the issue of gender inequality and bias must be removed in all countries, when such programs are in place at peace time it will significantly reduce the stigma and use of rape and gender-based violence in times of conflict.
2) Two, there must be a unified international response to ban the use of rape as a weapon of war once and for all, and thus strategies of prevention and awareness must be put into place, including in internally displaced persons and refugee camps and in times of post conflict.

3) Three, impunity must come to an end, or victims will continue to remain silent and not seek medical, psychological and legal attention if they feel there is no retribution or care for which they are safe to receive.

Something that the compulsive sex offender must know:

1. Sex, as great as it is, can never be a substitute for feelings of value and self-worth. Your sexual identity is critical but you are not your vagina or penis.
2. Relationships exist for mutual sharing not for bullying, coercing or dominating the will of another.
3. It is important to respect your partner's sexual choices and preferences.
4. Catering to your partner's sexual needs, as well as having your own needs met, is critical to a balanced relationship.
5. A difference in sex drive is not an excuse for infidelity; relationships must be built on compromise and trust from both individuals.
6. Your partner is not responsible for "giving you an orgasm". Your sexual climax is primarily dependent upon your own thinking and feelings about sex, as well as on the understanding of how your body responds.
7. Withholding displays of love and affection in an attempt to punish your partner is insensitive and immature.
8. Withholding sex or using it as a reward or promise for "good behaviour" demeans the significance of the act to you and your spouse.
9. Expecting 'sex-on-demand' at all costs and fuming or pouting if is not had, is childish behaviour which is completely unattractive and is likely to negatively impact your marriage.
10. An addictive/compulsive dependence on sex, may signal a need for counselling or therapy.
11. Kindness and thoughtfulness, as genuine displays of affection, can be the most powerful precursors to a sexually satisfying relationship.

Chapter 3

Now the sexual terrorist doesn't actually hold a weapon to your head to have sex; at least not a physical one. Through the use of "emotional weapons" like overt demands, manipulations, angry complaints, put downs, threats, and the withdrawal of attention/affection; sexual terrorists attempt to control the sexual relationship so as to ensure that their every sexual demand is met. In an extreme scenario, violence could also be used. The sexual terrorist is more obsessed with his/her own needs than with a relationship which focusses on meeting the needs of their partner. Now before you accuse me of being a backward thinker, I have no problem with sexual assertiveness or with the celebration of individual sexuality. I am not suggesting that it is not important to desire sexual pleasure and fulfilment but if sex is all that defines a relationship what will happen if or when that desire starts to wane? Moreover, if sex is going to be all about one individual's needs at the expense of another's happiness, why don't people just masturbate and call it a day?

Sexuality in our postmodern age has most decidedly taken on an assertive have-my-needs-met-at-all-costs bent which screams at us from the covers of most magazines. While in some respects this may be great and should guard against things like sexual abuse in relationships, as with any new movement, too far-east, is usually west. Yes, I am most definitely all for personal empowerment and the like but as a counsellor and observer of human behaviour, I am seeing a quality which for the purposes of our discussion I will name "sexual terrorism."

Without having to fully dissect the topic of masturbation, some of us know intuitively that as instructive as some may tout masturbation to be, it could never be enough. The experience of sexual release does not take care of the problem of relational loneliness and the desire for meaningful human connection. So why don't the sexual terrorists among us get this? To be fair, some of us may just have been born with a selfish streak, which turns up, guns blazing, in our intimate relationships. Others may have had failed sexual encounters in the past which sort of "spoiled" them and made them intent never to be left wanting again. Others, through poor modelling, may just believe that being sexually assertive means catering to "Numero uno". Some with deeper emotional issues may even use sex as a form of escapism, resulting in obsessive/compulsive/addictive sexual behaviour. This can take its toll on the other partner who may lack sleep or adequate rest, as a result of these seemingly unquenchable demands.

Perpetrators utilize sexual violence in conflict situations for many different reasons. Rape can be used as a method of ethnic cleansing, as was seen in the Bosnian War. Serbian fighters raped Muslim women to produce Serbian offspring and thereby "cleanse" the population. During the Sudanese War, however, the Janjaweed militia typically used rape as a scare tactic to humiliate, intimidate, and punish the non-Muslim women and communities. Colombia rival groups as well have been using rape and murder as part of a punitive code to strengthen control in specific regions.

Not only is rape considered the most invasive of war crimes, it has long-lasting consequences for entire communities and countries. Sexual violence during conflicts has contributed to the spread of HIV/AIDS and other sexually transmitted diseases in multiple regions. In addition, mass rape has produced a new generation of young adults that are growing up with only one parent or as orphans because their mother was killed during the conflict. This has long-lasting ramifications for countries that will only be seen in the coming decades as this generation reaches working and reproductive age.

Sexual terror and atrocities are crime of convenience, so the society needs to eliminate convenience to kill crime, for it to actually happen, the Person holding constitutional post in each country needs to take bold initiatives and pragmatic measures to amend constitution and make jurisdiction stronger.

Not just counting the number of incidents of gruesome crimes such as rape of man and woman, rape use as weapon of war, to get insight into the complexities and for better understanding of the reasons behind worldwide terror, sexual violence and even bigger human concern the reasons behind communal discord and hate crimes in so many different parts of the world, many outrageously pressing questions to ask, as in, What are those uncanny reasons behind unprecedented high degree of violence and war? Who is interested and who benefits the most from so much human bloodshed? Why and how are such heinous crimes committed? Who are those self-seeking people responsible? What are the motives of those perverts committing such inhuman crimes? People who perpetrates such crimes their actions are beyond human comprehension! To find out answers for all these contentious but seriously important questions and issues of significant importance for the entire humanity, we have to go into deep detail of human history, thoroughly analysis of past and present

political policies to gain comprehensive understating for reasons and causes behind profound crimes against humanity; why some mindless and heartless individual people makes such critical mistakes of harming other humans? Why such deadly crimes so brazenly are being committed?

The job of political leadership is to provide safety and security and sincerely work to unite citizens of their respective country, also the most challenging responsibility of political leadership governing the country is to provide and create new avenues for younger demographic and women so as to have better jobs and business opportunities for people of their country, above all political leadership needs to honestly manage country's finances and make productive use of available resources, the judiciary system of each country needs to be unbiased and do justice for all, unprejudiced judiciary system in necessary to prevent discrimination of the vulnerable.

The other leadership is Religious leadership, for whatever this leadership or hierarchy is worth, the role of religious hierarchy should be to preach its followers the essence of *"love, tolerance and commitment for establishing social harmony and gender equality,"* the religious leadership is ideally supposed to educate its followers to have No Racial and religious bias and to have solemnly non-discriminative approach, without having any prejudice should serve the purpose of humanity.

Then there is Business leadership, the role of Business or corporate honchos should be to provide job and business opportunities to people or those deserving individuals based purely on their merits. The Business owners and managers needs to be Non-bias and delivers justice, equal and fair treatment to all its employees and business associates, the selection of candidates for the job should be on merit, the most deserving person or persons should be given jobs and any other types professional assignments.

But the fact is that none of them, either the "Political leaders nor the Religious hierarchy or the Business owners," meets general expectations, all these three class of leaderships have in past hundreds or thousands of years of recorded human history have **not** played a positive and constructive role.

The Political leaders belonging to any kind of political system whether "Autocratic, Monarchist or Democratic," Dictatorial or Communist/Socialist or be it Capitalist, politician affiliated to any form of political class is/are and always have been worried and concern about their own political constituency and dedicatedly worked for securing for themselves highest possible political position of power, astute power hungry politicians to remain in power they've for thousands of years divided people on "Racial, religious, linguistic or on communal lines," instead of working to unite people of their country, contrary to that they work to divide people, a divide and rule policy is what suits the political hierarchy.

The religious priests to remain supreme and relevant, hence cults and other religious priests belonging to various different religions have covertly or overtly but systematically for generations have relentlessly worked to cause considerable disharmony and disunity among common people by using "mind control techniques, deception and exploitation by imploring upon their followers to believe in their weird spiritual teachings, brainwashing techniques deliberately applied to make their followers superstitious and insular," the religious hierarchy belonging to almost every religion preaches its followers that our religion is better than every other religions. The cults and religious hierarchy have always thought its followers to believe that their religion is on the right path to move closer to "God," and to seek divine blessing, **Religious Prejudice is the worse type of Prejudice,** once a person/persons become prejudiced and starts disregarding every other religious beliefs, then, that is what creates a situation for heart-wrenching hatred crimes and civil disobedience.

In Business and corporate world Nepotism, favouritism and cronyism is wide spread. In most cases the real and deserving candidates are deprived, lucrative jobs or business assignments are rendered to people based on either his/her source of influence or his/her religious or racial affiliation. The business managers have to always keep in mind their commercial interest there is no room for emotions in business. But there is another perspective as well to understand compulsion of business owners because the Businessmen normally works and survives under duress and pressure exerted on them by the politicians and governmental bureaucracy. Businesses have to patronage the elite political class for their business survival, but, that's not all, the business bosses at times and in many places also have to deal with criminals, terrorist groups and the mafias, in some of the region of the world the mafias and criminal gangs seizes the opportunity and treats the large Corporates as mulching cow, and brazenly demands protection money, if corporate managements do not abide and refuses to pay ransom money to the criminals, the criminal gangs in frustration adopts brazen unconventional methods to put pressure on business owners and resorts to violent means like arson and looting as well kidnapping the top managers of companies and demands ransom money, so, it's never so easy for corporates to do business, basically in every part of the world the business honchos have to face many peculiar unprecedented challenges, to sustain in business and politics people have to make ridiculous compromises.

Who created whom? *Humans created God a figment of our imagination or god created human beings.* This is an issue that has always been and will always remain a matter of intense debate and discussions, but, what is true is that most among us, we the people in our life time waste enormous amount of our precious time thinking about talking about discussing about "God," In glum and glory in good times and bad times many people think of and talk of god and only god. Ironically even those folks who are non-believers, such individual people belonging to Atheist or Agnostic "school of thoughts" otherwise "rightfully or wrongfully" they disregard concept of God and rejects religious beliefs yet this section of the society the "**unbelievers**" end up spending considerable amount of their time in thinking, talking and debating about religions and god.

If god created humans, than, who created God? These are some hard-pressed questions for which no one has any precise answer.

One reason for the importance of this topic is because religions often make strong claims on people's allegiance, and universal religions make these claims on all people, rather than just a particular community. For example, Islam has traditionally held that all people owe obedience to Allah's will. Thus, it is probably inevitable that religious commitments will sometimes come into conflict with the demands of politics. But religious beliefs and practices also potentially support politics in many ways. The extent and form of this support is as important to political philosophers as is the possibility for conflict. Moreover, there has been a growing interest in minority groups and the political rights and entitlements they are due. One result of this interest is substantial attention given to the particular concerns and needs of minority groups who are distinguished by their religion, as opposed to ethnicity, gender, or wealth.

Polytheism or Monotheism, Pagan's or Abrahamic, every religion has the history of dividing civil societies, religions are pitched against religions every religion wittingly tries its best to prove their point, that, theirs is the best religious belief and every other religion are inferior in perception to their religion, such tussle to prove their religious supremacy ends up bitterly dividing people and deeply polarizing the civil society, therefore, there is a popular perception, that, religions holds back progress in boosting the country's economic growth and in developing much needed civic and public infrastructure for the convenience of the people. Economic progress comes with social unity.

Its widely observed, that, great Peoples affinity and emotions are always with their own "Race, Religion, ethnicity and in some cases with their spoken language or the region they belong too," little do they care or think about the benefit of humanity, there are such brazen inhuman instances where the Man prejudice against woman, wherein men discusses among themselves and says, it is ok to flirt and seduce women of other religious communities but always respect girls and women belonging to our own community. I've heard from sources about some people's sly motives, for example some people believes "like there's nothing wrong in selling Narcotics Drugs to people belonging to other religious communities, it's perfectly ok to sell drugs and other banned substances to folks belonging other communities, but prevent youngsters of our own religion/community from consuming Drugs." Mindless affinity for their own Religion makes a person evil sometimes.

We need to have both global perspective as well as ground level perspective.

Bad Economic and Political policies becomes extreme cause of pain to large global populations. In modern era we have two types of political and economic system "the Socialist and Capitalist."

After the end of second world war emerged the two major Economic power centres the "United States of America and China," while Americans have adopted liberal and democratic political systems but their economic system is bizarre combination of both socialist and capitalist systems. In contrast the Chinese have adopted a very unique system to govern their country theirs is extreme communist/socialist political system while their economic system since the 1990's has been extreme **Capitalist**.

Flawed and reckless economic policies causes excruciating and irreparable damage to both social structure in civil society as well it severely harms the natural environment and ecological system. Whether we talk about the Chinese or Americans or the European Union countries Economic Policies which they have adopted in the 21st century is far from satisfactory, irresponsibly planned insensitive business and economic policies has resulted in causing major social problems and have created gender inequality besides it has increased discrimination and hatred crimes in civil societies. The gap between the rich and poor has widen substantially. The uncertain times have become even more uncertain, the reckless **printing of money** or to say frequent dose of economic stimulus package by the prominent industrialized nations like U.SA, Japan, China and Europe to boost their flagging economies after the infamous 2008 financial meltdown, lack of creative ideas and thoughts, instead the **Central Bankers** of prominent countries have found simple and easy way out that is to print unprecedented amount of Cash-currency notes for the purpose of creating artificially high cash liquidity in the banking system and tempt businesses and common-people to borrow more money for spending on buying consumer goods and to spend money on other extraordinary purchases.

The increase demand for industrial goods creates incessant demand for minerals and petroleum crude oil, and to meet rising demand for oil & gas, new technology has been invented in the 21st century called fracking to produce **Shale Oil**, the fracking technology that brutally cracks the rocks beneath the surface of the earth to pump out crude oil and gas, outrageously environment unfriendly fracking technology has caused profound harm to the environment, over mining digging the surface of the Earth deeper and deeper to extract minerals and pumping out crude oil has destroyed global environment and has dangerously unbalanced the ecological system, the weather and climatic condition around the globe is becoming more and more erratic and dreadful, due to which the world is experiencing frequent brutal natural disasters, causing unprecedented loses to public lives, properties and livelihood.

The mantra of 21st century to spur Economic growth is to create unprecedented amount of cash liquidity into the banking system, the **Central bankers** as a first step will reduced Key bank lending rate to 0%, if reducing interest rate to 0%

fails to have desire impact on country's economic growth than the next measure Central bankers will announce stimulus economic package in which they'll print *Billions of dollars of cash-currency notes* for indefinite period of time and if that as well fails to spur economic growth and comprehensively fails to bring down ever so high underunemployment rate, than, taking extreme step forward will reduce bank's key interest rate below 0%, that means **Negative interest rates**, so Negative interest-rate policy means the depositors instead of receiving interest income on the money they deposit with banks either earns no interest income or worst still the depositors have to pay banks interest or to say penalty per month to park their money with banks, those days are gone at least in leading industrialized nations, when people use to deposit their money and cash savings with banks and other government supported financial institutions and earn assured monthly interest income, or to say the **Fixed-income** market has been decimated, people are forced to take risk, common-people are lured and compelled to borrow more and spend more, which is extremely dangerous sign, Capitalists economic system has made stock-markets and commodity-markets a **casino**, people are left with little or no choice but to speculate on risky financial instruments and gamble with their money to earn money, such flawed and faulty economic policies as well are seriously responsible for increased crime and suicide rates around the world, also responsible for rising intolerance and hate crimes and religious extremism and terrorism.

Who is/are bigger and dangerous threat to humanity? Who is actually destroying our **planet earth**? Islamists terrorists or the Central bankers. Islamic terrorism of course is serious problem but much more brutal and seriously harming humanity is reckless and irresponsible economic and monetary policies.

New generation needs new solutions, but, how and who will give youngsters of new generation emphatic and practical solutions? But, even for the practical solutions to be more effective, new generation or rather every coming generation also needs to ensure that they develop modern and liberal thought process and needs to be more secular in their approach. Significantly large percentage world's population even in modern era of Digital age have primitive era mind-set, such folks are extremely superstitious in their belief and have insular thought process, hence they lack in confidence, on the flip side, there are also significantly large number of people around the world who firmly believe in living with the time and periodically keep making adjustment with their characteristics, so, the folks who in real terms are more practical and assertive in their approach towards life, such people will never wait for things to happen but will make things happen, high on confidence they will create opportunity for them rather than wait for someone else to provide them chance and opportunity.

Time is changing and so we must change as well, I call it evolving situation! But even as we have moved ahead from ice –age to stone- age and now we are living in 21st century in digital age, but, yet most people despite living in modern era and in contemporary times still have age old thinking process, majority of people are not adaptive.

Peace, progress, pleasure and prosperity will be achieved, when those craving for better standard of living starts accepting challenges that life throws at them, with pragmatic thoughts and creative ideas, courage to strive and determined execution of those creative and innovative ideas, the fruit lies in executing the ideas you have in your mind and not by simply discussing and debating your thoughts and ideas.

Uncertain times are becoming even more uncertain, corruption has become like an incurable cancer entire population of the world is impacted by high level of rampant corruption, which has also become cause for increasing hatred crimes in most parts of the world.

In this modern era, in this day and time in this digital age, the young generation craving for fascinating lifestyles, for the younger generation to achieve their objectives, what is required is "Not" the quantity of academic qualification but quality of **Cognitive and Technical skills**, the graduation courses and Master's degrees have or are becoming less significant, to survive and to live life with dignity and to thrive in this era and in this digitize world, young generation folks need to become more innovative and learn creative thinking technics which will enable them to adapt to change more easily, that's what will improve their future prospects and will make their future safe secure and profitable, and they'll be able live a comfortable life.

Here to prove a point I would like to mention few exemplary names of high achievers and incredible professional success story, the likes of "Bill Gates founder of Microsoft, Sam Walton founder of Walmart group, Steve Jobs promoter of Apple Computers and Mark Zuckerberg founder and promoter of the most successful and prolific Social media network "Facebook" all these glorious names have registered themselves in history books as legend and are epitome of amazing strive and thrive success story, but, all of these four examples that I've mentioned also have one thing in common as they succeeded in establishing major business conglomerate, their success had less to do with their academic qualification, but they are/were visionary and had creative ideas and innovative skills which they so overwhelmingly and resolutely executed and above all they had strong resolve and determination to achieve their objectives in life.

This piece of advice is Not for **Weak hearted** risk averse people, but, for those "**Brave-hearts**" who believe in taking that odd Risk in life, to achieve our goals in life just do not bother yourself thinking and planning moves and actions, simply move ahead with your decision that you think will potentially shape-up your future, so take a step forward and make your life the best experience, move on do not to hesitate and worry about any type of Legal Implication or Social Consequences, if Conventional methods fails, there is no harm in trying Un-Conventional methods, but don't give up without trying, just move ahead and execute your ideas, you bother only about implementing your ideas you have, don't simply waste time contemplating and discussing your thoughts, instead you motivate yourself, power your vision by this famous saying "*luck favours the brave,*" as most often it is seen, "*the goal of keeping our head float above water only ends up sinking us,*" live life not simply to survive but to thrive.

We see it in Movies, our favourite hero plays fiction role to solve fictitious problems. So, what do we do in our real life? Throw others out of business to stay in business, is it ethically fair thing to do? Should we? For our own survival we ruin other people's career prospects, well, maybe not or maybe correct, but, than as our purpose in life is, as we are born to compete with others, hence, for example: to win the race, we have to be focussed fully on reaching the finishing line first before anyone else, because in our business and professional life we have to be ready to accept many challenges, therefore, there's little that we can do but be fully focussed on securing our own victory, ethics and morality can dither us from achieving our desirable objectives in life.

Don't let chaos scare you, instead in difficult times as well, you be focussed on your business, think and care about serving your customers and clients.

Very important to note: Always be **Assertive**, Never ever be **Aggressive**, your assertiveness will send positive signal to your Clients/Customers and also to your business and professional competitors and Rivals, whereas being aggressive will turn your friends into foe, and will make your professional and business rivals your most bitter enemy. Always be in the habit of fulfilling your commitments even at the cost of you suffering personal loss or no matter how big a sacrifice you have to make. Not fulfilling commitments may possibly not harm us but it significantly harms the whole mankind, because people who suffers from betrayal, loses faith in humanity.

Defeat teaches us many lessons, provided we are ready to learn from our past mistakes, victory at times makes triumphant-person complacent, hence, a bit of advice for those folks who have in the past suffered failures and experience defeats, they should try to recoup and keep the disappointment of previous defeat at bay, and instead energise themselves and vehemently move ahead in life to accept the next challenges, never run away from accepting challenges.

Success and failures are part of everyone's life, hence there's no harm in trying and failing in your attempt to achieve your goals and objectives in life, rather than, **Not** trying at all to achieve your goals and objectives in life, because assuming and pre-empting fearful thoughts and feelings in mind thinking you will again fail in your endeavour. We must graciously learn to accept our failures. So, don't allow few chaotic incidents to halt your progress, remove all obstacle that are in the way preventing you from succeeding, there's no shame in Failing.

Don't be too hard on yourself. There are plenty of people willing to do that for you. Love yourself and be proud of everything you do, Even mistakes mean you are trying.

Common Sense is like a Deodorant, The People who needs it most Never use it.

Chapter 4

What are the root causes of terror and the reasons behind brutal crimes committed against women and children in particular? One has to deliberate a lot to find out the facts, because the reasons are far too many, as in, why humans display such wicked attitude and behaviour in carrying out heinous crimes without any hesitation?

People often see images of events, listens to news and stories of chaos or destruction and they start to irresponsibly react to what they see and or listen from others, seldom or rarely we'll find any such rightful thinking people who like to really go into the deep details of things to find out what really the truth of the matter is.

There is a difference between "**Reacting and Responding**" when you "React" you allow your External Circumstances Call shots, when you "Respond" Actions and Feelings, distinguish and draws Distinction.

Let's us understand and study the deep reasons and the nitty-gritty by touching base with some harsh realities, as in, what are those various links that creates circumstances which seemingly links with the section of people who commits such heinous crimes like rape, sexual terror assault and coerce young minor girls and boys into having sex? How "**politics of terror**" works? What is, if at all, there exist a nexus between "Religion, Politics and Terrorism?

21st century began on a very chaotic note, to begin with the world witnessed the so-called "Dotcom" bubble burst in the year 2000, when the companies in the business of "Internet, telecommunication & information Technology" experienced major decline in their fortune and fell on extreme hard times, the Stock-markets across the world collapsed, almost every company which were in the business like "Internet services, telecommunication, computing hardware and software" had to resort to purge. Many businesses were shut and millions of people around the world lost their jobs.

But the worse was to follow the next year in 2001, now prominently entered in the history books, the incident of terror attack on American soil on sept-11, called "9/11," Islamist terrorist outfit Al-Qaeda led and inspired by Osama-Bin-Laden launched a massive terror attack right in the heart of prominent US cities like New York, which devastated the Americans and shocked the whole world. The reaction was inevitable an obvious aggressive response, America's act of reprisal and retribution, incumbent U.S. president "**Mr George W Bush**" got good enough reason to blast the terrorist camps based in Islamic countries, the 9/11 terror attack became a catalyst for USA and its allies to wage war on terror. US president first in 2001 ordered his <u>military forces</u> to attack terrorist bases inside Afghanistan and one year later another war started when US president Mr George W Bush took decision to dislodge the monstrous Iraqi dictator **Saddam Hussein** from power, in the month of "March 2003" US army forces with full force marched inside Iraq and attacked Iraqi army and overthrew Saddam's regime from power.

For the first time after nearly an 8 decade long pause, first time ever after the fall of the great Islamic power centre the mighty **Ottoman Empire**. The Islamic militancy emerged in its new avatar in full elements. The emergence of 21st century has seen the whole new form of **Sunni-Islamic Terror** unleashed on the world, a strong resilient violent force became unrestrained, not just America but Islamic terror has taken centre stage on full global stage, in 21st century almost every country has directly or indirectly felt the pain and tremor of Islamic jihadist terrorism.

The prominent Sunni Islamic jihadist terrorist groups names that have become a household name like the "Al-Qaeda, Boko Haram, Al Nusra, Chechnya based Terrorist, Afghan based "Taliban," and the most dreadful of all the terrorist is "**ISIS**" (Islamic state of Iraq and Al-Sham also known as Islamic State)," these are some of the Islamic jihadist extremist groups which has terrorise the whole world. Islam has many faction and denominations but each of the many faction of Islam is directly linked to the two prominent **sect** of Islam **Shiite** and **Sunni**, Islam is a divided religion and has two main rival faction Shia and Sunni, now each of the above mentioned names of jihadist terrorists groups have direct affiliation with Sunni Islam, yes, all the jihadist elements and terrorist groups follow Sunnis Islam, the jihadi army represent Sunni-Islam, however the Sunni-Muslims in public will always try to distance themselves from the jihadists.

The prime objective of Islamic extremist owing allegiance to Sunni Islam is what the founder of Islam had preached in his sermons, which is to expunge every other non-Sunni Islam religion and also the atheist or scientific belief from the world and establish hard-core Islamic Sharia law all over the world, by establishing Islamic Caliphate the world over.

It has become a major, defining moment for those who pursue political and social propaganda.

The Sunni – Islam is in head-on confrontation with the rest of the world's regions and religions, the Sunni Muslim are recklessly and frivolously fighting a multi-dimensional war for no apparent reason. A lot of bloodshed could easily be avoided and large world population can live in peace and unity provided the age old barbaric Islamic doctrine is discarded.

Politics makes strange bedfellows, politics is an art of making impossible matters possible, politics is not a profession for faint minded or weak hearted individuals, the mathematics of politics always adds up to "2+2=5" and not "4," politics is the game best left to be played by those men and women who are strong minded and have aggressive approach and those who are callous and work with sly motives in dealing with contentious issues concerning broader demographics and every other regional matters. Politicians needs to be crafty in their manoeuvring and narcissistic in pursuing their nefarious motives.

All Muslims are not terrorist "agreed" but, do all Muslims sincerely oppose and condemn Islamic terrorists and terrorism? The answer would perhaps be a big "NO," yes, that's because none of the prominent Muslim ruled country's Governments never ever sincerely regret Islamic terrorist activities, also none of the oil rich gulf nations like the "Saudi Arabia, Qatar, Kuwait etc have never ever come forward to vociferously and vehemently condemn the brutal atrocities and violence of the various Islamic jihadist terrorists groups. Instead there are occasions when few of the prominent Muslim personalities give vague and peculiar reason to justify the heinous crimes the extremist jihadist so outrageously commits. When "No" prominent Islamic nation, scholars and eminent individuals from Muslim community sincerely oppose or condemn the terrorist activities of the Islamic jihadist forces, that's what infuriated the non-Muslim communities of the world, hence the social and economic gap and gulf between the Muslims and Non-Muslims only gets ever so wide. Which is also perceived as "Islamophobia."

Even if at all in public to avoid backlash and social isolation some Muslims shun the jihadists terrorist violence and say that jihadists are un-Islamic and true Islam is peace and non-violent, and those Muslims indulging in terror and are killing innocent people are evil and not real Muslims, but such views and reaction of Islamic folks are mere ploy and tactics to divert attention, in reality based on empirical evidence and historic records proves that violence and terrorism is intrinsic linked to Islam, terrorism is culture of Sunni-Islam.

Propagandist mainly from Muslim community have always worked overtime to propagate propaganda and graciously projects Islam as religion of peace, well, maybe their intent is or was sincere, however the records speaks a different story. Islam as religion of peace and its founder Prophet Mohammed have very well been Branded as Allah's (so-called name of Muslim God) last apostle and messenger of peace. Again the historic records "vis a vis" the attributes and activity of Islam and the followers and believers of the faith Islam loudly and perspicuously speaks and activities of Muslims proves that Islam is everything but peaceful religion, ever since Islam was invented, the Islamic folks to achieve their objective to spread Islam targeting all the demographic throughout the world, they have resorted to violence means, preached and practice hatred against every other religion and spiritual beliefs. Islam is not religion of peace but of destruction.

Islam as we know was established by Prophet Mohammed (the last prophet), Mohammed was an absolute illiterate man, but as some historians have said about him is, that, prophet Mohammed was extremely clever and astute person, very cunning in his manoeuvre.

Whatever the critics of Islam may talk or write about Islam, but one thing is certain that, Islam since the time it emerged on the global scene, it has gained considerable power in global arena and has moved forward from strength to strength to become the most powerful and fearful religion. Who should be credited for the rise of Islam? Yes, someone has to be credited for making Islam albeit not progressive but yes the most prosperous religion. The credit goes to the Islamic council ministers and office bearers of medieval time, yes, the success of Islam is largely because it has been very well planned and branded and marketed.

Indeed Islam was very well promoted with excellent marketing tools, the managers of Islam whoever they may have been have very well branded the image of their *prophet Mohammed the founder of Islam and his legacy*. The excellent Branding, packaging and marketing has what made Islam a phenomenal success, even the harshest and bitter critics of Islam can't deny this fact, the bitter critics of Islam can't deny the fact as to how a good branding and promotion has helped Islam in establishing itself as most powerful religion in the world, also one should take a leaf out of the book and must learn a lesson about the fact that branding and marketing not only helps businesses in selling their consumer products but even religions needs to be marketed for better success and which is to attract bigger crowd who are ready to believe every bit of nonsense that is told to them. The modern era bosses and managers of corporate world must applaud the marketing skills of those managers of Prophet Mohammed for making Islam and its founder a great success story. Else, fundamentally Islamic doctrine and philosophy is ridiculously horrible and full of insular belief, propagating violence and cruelty.

Islam is the most misunderstood religion, the followers of Islam, those people who support Islam and its founder, have misunderstood and misconstrued it.

Even the opponent and bitter critic of Islam those folks who hate Islam and its founder, have misunderstood and have misconstrued Islam.

Islam is the most misunderstood religion, neither its followers nor its opponents, none of them understands the basics of Islam.

In fact all three Abrahamic religions "Judaism, Christianity, Islam" are full of confusion and contradiction, while there is unanimity among them in belief that they follow the same one God theory (but each of these three religions addresses the same one god by different names), despite the fact, as they believe that prophet Abraham is father of Islam, Christianity and Judaism yet, these three brotherly religions have history of ferociously fighting and killing each other ever since they've come into existence. Islamic people goes a step further and calls both Jews and Christians **Kafirs** (infidels), Muslims do not stop just at calling Christians and Jewish Kafirs but they further says that **Allah** (name of Islamic God) made serious fundamental mistakes while creating the Jewish and Christians the people who follow Judaism and Christianity are flawed and ugly creation of god and **not** worth calling humans, therefore *"fire of hell for Jewish and Christians"* and because Muslims are the best creation of god and are purest hence *paradise in heaven for Muslims*.

How silly "any logic"?, if we take a deep look inside history books, we'll find that Islam is more confusing and full of contradiction, because the founder of Islam prophet Mohammed himself was man of double standards, he was man of peace and integrity as well as epitome of cruelty and destruction, he was pro feminist as he gave few fundamental rights to women but on the flip side he had also tried to tied down women and labelled them inferior to men, his most controversial support for stoning women to death and giving rights to men saying its ok if the husbands flog their wife/wives for the spouse misconduct.

One incident I would like mentioning to prove the so-called messenger of peace prophet Mohammed's (Allah's apostles) abhorrent attributes: in one of the many war which Mohammed fought in 7th century to establish Islam "At the Massacre of Khaybar, Muhammad brutally tortured a Jewish chieftain for extracting information about where he had hidden his treasures. When the treasure was uncovered, the chieftain was beheaded. This chieftain was the husband of the most beautiful Jewish woman of Khaybar, the 17-year-old Safiyaah. Safiyaah's family members had been annihilated by Muhammad at the Banu Qurayza massacre. Now having beheaded her husband, the Prophet took Safiyah as his sex-slave and copulated on the same night." Another incident: "In the massacre of the Jewish Settlement of Bani Mustaliq, Muhammad captured their women and took twenty-year-old Jewish girl, Juwayriya as his sex-slave."

(here again to remind you folks, who are not well verse with the history of Islam, that is, that, Islam is bitterly divided in two faction "Shia and Sunni" and all the jihadist terrorist groups that have so severely terrorised the world belongs to or owes allegiance to Sunni Islam, the Sunni's for generations have suppressed and oppressed the minority Shias)

If some people think, what has the religion, got to do with Branding, Public-Relationship, Image- Makeover, Marketing, well, they need to think again. Not just or only the Celebrities like Sporting personalities, Movie Stars, Corporates, Businesses and Politicians require Branding and promotion and marketing services to promote themselves and their ideologies or their products, but even religions and cults as well needs to work unrelentingly and tirelessly to promote their belief for them to win the trust and support of people.

The perfect example are the phenomenal success of Islam and Christianity, yes, both these Abrahamic religions are quintessential perfect example of "Branding and "Good' Public relationship" and strategic sales & marketing of their religious ideologies. The council and office-bearers of both Islam and Christianity have done an excellent work in promoting their beliefs as well as branding of their alleged founders of their respective religions "Mohammed and Jesus," that's how they've succeeded in gaining unflinching support of people from around the world. In contrast the other great ancient religious beliefs like the Paganism and Judaism have faded away, maybe because their religious leadership may have become complacent and frivolous.

But, we should be fair in our assessment of the ground level realities and we need to establish the truth of every religion, simply not put the entire blame for heinous crimes and atrocities on Islam and its follower, exemplary sentencing may discourage the violent minority, let us not simply blame Islam for all the social ills, the critics may argue to prove their point that Islam is the most monstrous and brutal religion, but their apparently exist many other religions as well, the most prominent among many religions are "Buddhism, Christianity & Hinduism among many more other smaller religious communities, and make no mistake, please do not ignore the harsh facts that each of these religions and many of their believers and followers as well carry the tag and stigma on their head of practicing extreme brutal crimes and atrocities, crime against women and children, not to simply make Islam and its followers a scapegoat, and allow other religions to cleverly brush their sins under the carpet.

Every religion boast about them and argues that the USP of their religion is Peace, Integrity and Tolerance, but the record of almost all of the most prominent religions proves that each of the religions have major short-comings, each of the major religions are marred by violence and hatred, if we take a deep look into Buddhism, most of the Buddhist ruled and dominated countries have dismal record of peace and integrity, we've seen in many Buddhist countries such as Vietnam, Cambodia, Burma, in these countries in the past, rift between political ideologies and sharp differences among top politicians and religious leaders have resulted in some of the most horrible and bloodiest conflict, particularly the Vietnam civil war in the 1960's was heart-wrenching, the other strong predominately Buddhist country Korea had immediately after the end of 2nd WW had plunged into most destructive and outrageous civil war which ultimately divided the nation in North – South Korea, beside that the aggressive invasion of Japan in China and Japanese soldiers atrocities against Chinese in 1930s and 40s, than China's own history of extensive bloody civil wars and internal conflicts, all grave violation of human rights.

The European population which largely consist of Christianity, the notorious European crusaders largely belonging to Christian/Catholic faith, had for centuries ransacked the lucrative resource rich African and south-American countries, millions of black Africans were killed their properties looted and were made slave and were mercilessly forced to convert to Christianity, same thing happen in resource rich south & north-America wherein the native Americans and red-Indians were brutally tortured and killed and forced to convert into Christianity, something similar happened in another resource rich territory of the world **Australia**, where to gain control of the invaluable and massively wealthy land of Australia the Europeans shamefully killed according to some estimates nearly 2 million **aborigines** the original habitants of Australia and finally the Europeans took over the whole Australian nation under their control.

But the most inhuman crimes that were committed in Nazi ruled Germany (predominately Christian country) and in other German ruled European countries during the 2nd WW, where the people belonging to Jewish community were pushed into Gas Chambers to die and their bodies were then brutally torn apart, the skin of death Jewish Holocaust victims were sent to the leather tanneries to be used to make leather product such as bags and shoes, and the bones of Holocaust victims were allegedly used in making handicraft. Such is the history of the crimes so ruthlessly committed by the Europeans.

Call them Pagans or Heathens or Hindus, yes, Hinduism is also a big religion, even though Hindus a spread across the whole world and are in sizeable majority in many nations, but the biggest congregation of <u>Hindu population</u> is based in India, ever since the **Aryans** (Indo- European' race or group of people) invaded India some Four Thousand or so years ago. The Pagans or call them Hindus has bitterly divided themselves into various social class and formed caste system, there is bi-polar division amongst the Hindus, the upper-caste & lower-caste Hindus, for centuries the upper-caste Hindus have brazenly and inhumanly humiliated and discriminated the lower caste Hindus, such has been atrocities against the lower caste Hindus by their upper-caste rivals, that the

Upper-caste Hindus have treated their lower caste peer worse than dogs and cats, particularly vulnerable have been the lower caste Hindu women, there have been instances and which have for thousands of years happen on recurring bases that the lower caste Hindu women at times are sexually exploited and at times are **paraded Naked** on in streets in villages by the upper-caste Hindus.

Like Muslims are radicalized so are the Hindus, yes, even the Hindus are radicalized by the Hindutva (fundamentalist Hindu organizations) minded organization and political parties to gain political power, the right-wing Hindu political parties have systematically cause deep and comprehensive division among the civilian population, they've communally polarized the large Indian population (divided' Majority Hindu's on one side and minority Muslims and Christians on the other-side) and have done so successfully.

Similarly like there are terrorist in Islam, so are there bloodthirsty extremists among Hindu religion as well, but, the Hindu terrorism is of different type, much different from Islamic terrorists, the Hindu terrorism works subtly and discreetly and with sly motives, unlike Islamic terrorist groups who are very ostentatious in displaying their aggression, and the Islamic jihadist terrorist always come forward and take responsibility of the crimes and explosive blast they commit, but contrary to Islamic type of terrorism. The bosses of Hindu extremists groups are clever and cunning, they never make their intention and motives known public, the Hindu terrorism have master the art of passing the blame of their nefarious activities on others, and their nefarious activities includes crimes like orchestrating communal riots, rapes, explosive blast at public places or at religious places, particularly the Hindu terrorist organizations always manage to successfully pass the blame of the perpetrated crimes committed on the head of Muslims, the Hindu terrorist have always made Muslims scapegoat, they hit two birds with one stone, they successfully manage to gain public sympathy from people of their own Hindu communities as well as they manage to disparage the image of Muslims and Islam, hence by polarizing Indian society and radicalizing vulnerable Hindu youngsters, the Political party affiliated to Hindu extremist groups becomes direct beneficiary and gains political power, divisive forces plays divide and rule political game in India.

Basically what the Hindu extremist and miscreant groups hierarchy does is that they hire contract killers belonging to Muslim community, pays handsome amount of money to Islamic jihadists type of terrorist or criminals to carry out bomb blast at key Hindu dominated locality or they pay large amount of money to some miscreant criminals belonging to either community and orchestrate communal riots which are mostly or always between Hindus and Muslims, hence, what always happens is that the Muslims are blamed for all types of terrorist activities that happens in most part of India, this how Muslim population is stigmatized and the civilian population gets ferociously polarize on communal lines.

What helps the right-wing Hindu extremist groups is the role of Indian Media, the inept and corrupt media (both' Print and Electronic media) plays significant role in propagating the right-wing extremist Hindu propaganda, also because the private media in India is largely owned and controlled by radical Hindu business families, so, media plays critically important role in helping spread bias political and communal message of right-wing Hindu political party, glorifying extremist Hindu ideologies.

Sharp differences on religious issues among several important religions of the world often fuelled bitter power struggles for political control of the land, which occasionally erupts into violence and bloodshed. The terrorist attacks of September 11, 2001 were a rude awakening for the Western world. It suddenly seemed like the conflict between capitalism and communism had only delayed a more serious and potentially devastating three-way battle between Christian beliefs, Islamic beliefs, and secular democratic materialism, with each region of the world having its own cultural investments to protect.

A fierce debate is now raging between Christians, Muslims, and secular intellectuals in the world media and on the Internet. And if the American invasion of Iraq has taught us anything, it is that we must expect the political and religious tensions to continue to rise over the coming decades, with increased military spending, an escalation in global conflict, and the possibility of nuclear terrorism. Our interpretation of the history of ideas and beliefs began around three thousand years ago, when the Jewish priesthood took advantage of the newly discovered power of alphabetic writing to craft a detailed mythology about a single God of creation. Using myths about miracles, the priests succeeded in uniting their population under a single belief and giving them a practical set of laws and values. Guided by their communal faith, the Jewish people themselves became the law-keepers, and under the watchful eye of a powerful priesthood, kings were held accountable to the same standards as commoners. Greek storytellers also adopted alphabetic writing, but they were unable to make their traditional myths about a family of selfish gods sound convincing, and interaction between the gods was often unfriendly, and so Greek religious morality was largely ineffective.

So, it is the Hebrew or Jewish people who innovated and introduced then hard sold the concept of belief that there is *just one God* and who is super natural and divine and has created every species as well is the creator of the whole universe, and have unprecedented super-natural power and miraculously control each Humans destiny. The allege purpose behind concocting fake story and selling this concept of "single' God" by Jewish must have been a strategy to neutralise the power and rule of several Roman and Egyptian Pagan kings and rulers who use to believe in multiple gods and idol worshipping. Therefore both the most powerful religion of our time Christianity and Islam are offspring of Judaism, Christianity first then Islam are nothing else but born out of Judaism and have adopted the spiritual traditions and ideologies of Judaism and are plagiarised version of Paganism. But, ironically the selfish Islam and Christianity after coming into existence have done everything possible to eradicate Judaism from this world. At every nooks and corner on this planet earth Islam and Christianity have rigorously harassed the Jewish folks. Therefore I perhaps won't be wrong in saying, that, by introducing the concept of one God, *the Jewish folks perhaps, dig their own grave.*

Article titled: "The assortment of Christian Belief" stated: "From the beginning of human civilization priests and 'holy men' have invented pious nonsense. For the priesthood the rewards have been immense: power, prestige and wealth. They have fused with, and become part of, the ruling elite. But times of social stress have always seen the emergence of a counter-priesthood, radicals or fundamentalists, preaching a purity of fable; ascetics, puritans and fanatics who revile and castigate a corrupt and worldly religious establishment and offer themselves as apostles of Truth and Divine Wisdom.

Rome's 1st century colonisation and exploitation of Judaea placed huge stresses on a theocracy that had enjoyed absolute power under the Maccabean kings and had been placated and indulged even by Herod the Great. Pharisees on the one hand – rabbinic guardians of a religious correctness, not part of the Temple hierarchy– and Essenes on the other – egalitarian purists, who withdrew to their own communities and lived by their own rule – trained the cadres, and fashioned the earliest ideology, for a radical recasting of Judaism. A century of endemic rebellion, civil war,

and wars of national resistance, leading ultimately to catastrophic defeat, made ready the seed bed for a violent and profound religious revolution."----

Basically every religion have their own agenda, some make it known publically, and some religion prefers to keep their motives under wrap and agenda hidden, every major religion has a history of destructive past as well as present.

Racial or linguistic prejudice, particularly Religious prejudice, any types of prejudice makes a person feel insecure, whenever a person feels insecure his/her thoughts gets disturb and attention gets distracted, insecurity in a person makes the affected person paranoid, when paranoia sets in the mind of a person that's when he/she commits hatred crimes.

Do a thorough check of ancient history and establish the historic facts, you will discover, that, Both the most powerful religions of our time Islam and Christianity are flawed and full of contradiction, only hallow promises nothing of substance, just a clever ploy to **capture power** by exploiting the vulnerability of naïve and lunatics "unworldly individuals and foolish groups of people" who are in plenty all over the world, who are ready to believe anything and everything they are told to believe and do anything and everything they are asked to do, so, **Islam and Christianity are satanic fraud**.

Chapter 5

The 2nd world-war ended in September 1945, ever since the end WW II, the world has witness numerous wars, like the Korean war in 1950s, in the mid 1960's gruesome Vietnam war, the Iran – Iraq conflict in the 1980s and in the beginning of 21st century the U.S. – Iraq war that was fought to oust tyrant dictator Saddam from power.

But, after the end of 2 ferociously fought world wars in the twentieth century, the worse conflict of the 21st century started in the year 2011. The so-called

Arab-Spring revolution which apparently turned into full fledge Islamic sectarian war. The Arab spring conflict had initially started for humble purpose, fed-up of staying under the autocratic rule for thousands of years the people of many Islamic Arab countries started raising their voice demanding freedom from the brutal and callous dictators.

The people of Tunisia, Libya then Egypt first walked down the streets and city squares protesting against the misrule of their country's political leadership. Men and women both gender joined hands and unitedly started the call for revolution and freedom from autocracy and demanding rights for civil liberties, the western media termed the protest of Arab citizen for revolution and freedom as "**ARAB - SPRING**." But, No, sooner had the so-called Arab spring had stared with humble intention. The Islamic jihadist were quick to pounce on the opportunity, the militant Islamic jihadist quickly hijacked the whole concept and defeated the purpose of revolutionary protest which was started by humble common citizens of Arab nations belonging to every religions and community, the Islamist jihadist terrorist changed the dynamics of the Arab spring revolution, instead they gave a complete new meaning and dimension to the so-called Arab spring revolution.

The Islamic jihadist terrorist turn the Arab spring into unprecedented Arabs nightmare, the fundamentalist jihadist twisted the Arab Spring into major conflict, the conflict between the liberal and moderates minded folks versus the fanatics supporters of barbaric Islamic sharia laws, but not just that, the worse still, the Islamic jihadist turned the Arab spring into major confrontation between the two rival Islamic Sect, yes, the purpose of revolution was twisted, the various Islamic jihadist terrorist whose affiliation is with Sunni Islam, the jihadist turned the Arab Spring into major conflict between the two major Islamic Sect of "**Shia's and Sunni's**."

The Islamic Sunni terrorist groups several of them structured their own nefarious agenda, and they brazenly without any fear made their heinous agenda public, the Sunni militants set agenda was or is to make the entire Arabian peninsula countries free from every other religious groups including the Shia's and various offshoot communities with affiliation to Shia Islam, and the Christians, Kurdish, Jewish, Yazidis and every other minority religion, the Sunni jihadist terrorist want to establish a staunch Sunni Muslim caliphate all over the middle-east Arabian as well in most of African countries and later all over the World.

The Sunni Islamic terrorist groups gave an open call to every other religious faith, either to convert to Sunni Islam or Perish.

The middle-east political and social crisis that started in the year 2011 has plunge the entire Islamic world into chaos, there is near total political and social anarchy in most severely affected Arab and North-Africa's Muslim dominated countries, countries such as "Libya, Syria, Yemen and Somalia" have become failed states, Syria and northern parts of Iraq have become hell of the place to live in, Islamic countries that are situated far and further away from middle-east Arabian region such as Pakistan and Afghanistan are also experiencing grim political instability and social & civilian unrest.

Major rich affluent and powerful countries like China and Russia on one side, while America, Britain, French on the other side, while Russia is more perspicuously siding with Syria, the other countries like the USA and its allies are trying to do balancing act, whereas they can't be seen supporting Islamic jihadist at the same time USA and its allies the Germans and French can't allow Russia to establish its dominance in the Arabian region.

Surprisingly "Al-Qaeda" jihadist organization that once dominated the terror world, the same Al-Qaeda that shocked the world with horror when it blasted twin towers building structure right in the heart of America on September 2001 (9/11), but after the death of its founder and mentor "Bin –laden" the clout of Al-Qaeda seems to have subsided as its terrorist jihadist are not playing a dominant role in the Arab world social and political conflict that started in 2011.

The major terrorist organization that has emerge on the global centre stage are "Boko Haram and Al-Shabaab" are dominating terrorist activities in North & East-Africa region, however there are many fringe and big terror jihadist group that have devastated the Arabian countries but the most fearful and extremely brutal terrorist that ripped the Arab world and now it has even jolted the super power "USA," yes, the name of gruesome terrorist group is "**IS or ISIS (Islamic state of Iraq and Al-sham)**," ISIS has occupied the centre most stage as far as terrorist activities goes, the whole world is petrified and frets by the name of ISIS.

The most dreaded Sunni jihadist terrorist outfit the ISIS allegedly led by an Sunni Iraqi man "Abu Bakr al-Baghdadi" has notoriously and comprehensively terrified the world, the Sunni-Muslim jihadist terror group ISIS brutally slaughters Men, brazenly Rapes Women and girls, kidnaps foreign nationals, and executes the massacre of Iraqi and Syrian soldiers.

ISIS have served a severe blow to mighty super power America and has not hesitated in challenging the mighty super power nation USA and its allies."

The crude and ruthless ISIS jolted American political leadership and its people by killing two American journalist "James Foley and Steven Sotloff" both, these two American journalist who were on their professional duty, they were doing their professional duty of covering and reporting political and terror events that were happening in Syria and other neighbouring countries in the middle-east, when they were kidnapped in Syria by the ISIS terrorists and were kept captive for considerable period of time, ISIS had allegedly demanded ransom, but subsequently they (ISIS) remorselessly and mercilessly displayed their cruelty.

The ISIS in August 2014 first ferociously and inhumanly killed the kidnapped journalist "James Foley" then after a fortnight in September 2014 the ISIS terrorist killed the second kidnapped journalist Steven Sotloff, the ISIS had released video footage of the killing of both James and Steven on social media network, the video film allegedly showed and man fully covered in black attire holding sharp knife in his hand and mercilessly slaughtering beheading "James and Steven."

The man who supposedly executed the slaughtering act of both James and Steven is an alleged British national of Kuwaiti origin (later identified, his pseudo name "Jihadi John" his real name is "Mohammed Emwazi), the same man who slaughtered James and Steven also spoke in the recorded video, he threw an open challenge to the US president threatening the US and its allies of much more harsh measures and of dire consequences if they continue to interfere in Arabian political matters and if the US and its allies becomes or try's to become a stumbling block in terms of preventing the ISIS from achieving its objective of establishing Islamic caliphate in the Arabian and African countries.

The alleged involvement of a British national in butchering two young American journalist "James Foley & Steven Sotloff" sent shiver down the spine and alarm the western world particularly the Europeans, reports points out that most European countries became or has become a major sourcing point for the Islamic jihadist organization to recruit the young and adventurous audacious youths to fight jihad against the so-called infidels army, the staunch Islamic hard-line belief that all who do not believe in "Allah or their holy prophet Mohammed" are non-believers and infidels and Muslims are thought in their Islamic schools that the infidels are equal to Satan (evil) and killing the infidels or harming them is not a sin but their holy duty to honour the commitments of their prophet Mohammed.

But, the ink wasn't even dried yet, the media and political analyst were still debating the gruesome killings of two American nationals James and Steven, US president was cobbling up support and building coalition of the willing nations to attack the targets of the most dangerous jihadist Sunni terrorist hideouts of the ISIS, yet another worse incident occurred around the midnight U.K time on 13 September 2014, ISIS delivered another fatal blow, on late Saturday night 9/13/2014, on its website on social media the terrorist group ISIS released a video images showing the killing and this time it was turn of a 44 years-old British national David Haines. Sadly, David a Scottish British national was killed by the Islamic jihadist ISIS terrorist in the same manner the way the two American journo Foley and Sotloff were killed, David Haines as well was slaughtered and ruthlessly beheaded, allegedly by the same allege Britain based Jihadist ("Jihadi John" alias "Mohammed Emwazi) who had beheaded James and Steven.

David Haines was an aid worker a humanist who had devoted his life serving humans and was on his trip to the Mid-east for human cause, he was serving and helping the distressed and displaced Syrian refugee in the refugee camps, while he was working at the Syrian refugee camp, the terrorist kidnapped him and held him captive. The killing of David Haines by the ISIS terrorist was a warning and to stop Britain from helping the Kurdish fighters in north Iraq, worth noting is that, Islamic jihadist are involve in fierce battle with Kurdish arm Peshmerga forces to gain control of northern Iraqi territory.

"The inhuman killings of three blokes "James Foley, Steven Sotloff and David Haines" each citizens of prominent western countries by the ISIS terrorist that too in the span of 30 days, the purpose prima facie seems to be that the Islamic terrorist wanted to categorically express by their action of warning the world community that they cannot be bowed down by the strong worded Western-nations threat to degrade and decimate their jihadist movement and defeat them in their objective to establish Islamic caliphate based on barbaric Islamic Sharia laws. The ISIS leadership emphatically made its intentions clear to the western nations as well to those governments of Arabian countries who have pledged their support to the western countries like the US, French, Britain, that they (ISIS) are ready to fight it out against the formidable alliance forces."--- This could perhaps be the most diplomatic assessment and thinking of the political analysts community and the political commentators.

But to take more practical and pragmatic view in assessing, as in, why did the ISIS terrorist killed James Foley, Steven Sotloff and David Haines? What is the motive behind killing' was it religious? The ISIS have also made it clear that they are not willing to stop just at killing these 3 western gentlemen but warns that they will continue doing so, which means they intend killing more western nationals the same way if the U.S. and its allies don't stop confronting them (ISIS) in Syria and Iraq, so, if ISIS is doing what they are doing simply because they are religious people and love their religion and their prophet? These are loaded questions, in my opinion, the killings by the ISIS terrorists of foreign nationals and also threatening to continue to keep killing many more non-Muslims and westerners, whosoever becomes obstacle for them in achieving their motives. There is "**more to it than meets the eyes**," the ISIS terrorist organization can't survive for even a moment all by themselves unless they are patronize by some discreet power centre, obviously the ISIS jihadist terrorists are simply a pawn, they must be having some strongest political patronage and that political or perhaps a combination of political and business forces must be very potent.

The allege conspirators and manipulators with vested interest who must be playing crucial role in planning the terrorist activities of the ISIS, as the conspirator's purpose must be simply to polarize the world, divide the naïve frivolous section of the world's population on communal and religious ground, because more the people these jihadist organizations like Boko-Haram, Al-Shabaab, Al Qaeda and ISIS, will kill, the more atrocious they will be in their action and atrocities against common people belonging to non-Muslim as well as Non-Sunni Muslim factions of Islam, and the more hawkish these jihadist terror groups will sound, the more the gulf between the Sunni Islamic people and others will widen, that means the division between Islam and Non-Islamic people of the world, which apparently makes "**Islam versus the Rest Battle**."

Now moving on further with the same topic of **Beheadings**; even though we are living in 21st century, science and technology has made tremendous progress, yet, even in this digital age of Fast-computers and advance internet technology, the age old draconian practice of capital punishment by beheading humans still persist in many Arab countries and the territories which are under the control of hard-line Islamist fundamentalist jihadist (Islamic holy warrior) militants, countries such as Saudi Arabia and few other Muslim rule nations where allege offenders are beheaded if they are found guilty of committing 3rd degree crime. Without any fair trail of court proceedings, also bias and inefficient Police investigation, at times the real perpetrator of crime manages to skip punishment, instead innocent person wrongly gets indicted and faces consequence of severe punishment.

The use of **capital punishment in Saudi Arabia** is based on Sharia (or Islamic law) and is prominent internationally because of the wide range of crimes which can result in the death penalty and because it is usually carried out by public beheading. In 2011, the Saudi government reported 26 executions in the country. Unlike executions in most other countries that have not abolished the death penalty, executions of offenders are not performed privately in prisons, but publicly in central Riyadh, and have been called the "only form of public entertainment" in Saudi Arabia "apart from football matches."

Saudi Arabia has a criminal justice system based on a hard-line and literal form of Sharia law reflecting a particular state-sanctioned interpretation of Islam.

In one of such incident: Rizana Nafeek a young nanny from Sri Lanka, was beheaded by sword in January 2013 in Saudi Arabia, punishment for allegedly killing a baby in 2007 when she was believed to be just 17. The execution spurred international outcry, given Nafeek's age at the time of the incident and her limited access to a defence attorney. The beheading has also shined a light on the Arab kingdom's medieval system of punishment, which includes cutting the hands off thieves, executing women accused of adultery, and flogging men accused of being gay.

Few details of Nafeek's execution have leaked from the country's tightly controlled media, but the interior ministry said her head was severed from her body in public in Dawadmy, a dusty suburb of the capital Riyadh.

In modern times, women in Saudi Arabia condemned to death were traditionally executed by gunfire, but in recent years they have routinely been beheaded, an historic form of execution ordered under sharia, or the Muslim religious law that governs the country. The death penalty is routinely allowed for criminals convicted of murder, rape, armed robbery, drug trafficking or drug use, and apostasy or the renunciation of the Islamic faith, according to human rights group Amnesty International.

Some 82 executions were carried out in Saudi Arabia in the year 2012, according to Amnesty. It is unknown how many of them were women or carried out by sword, but the majority of the condemned were foreigners, like Nafeek. Beheadings in Saudi Arabia are governed by certain rules. They are conducted in public, typically in town squares or near prisons. The condemned, as well as the executioner, typically wear white. The convict is blindfolded, handcuffed and often given a sedative. A plastic tarp, several feet wide, is sometimes spread out around the convict to make cleaning up the blood and recovering her head easier.

Another gruesome incident that happen in Syria: Jihadists in Syria kidnapped a Catholic priest in the Idlib area and beheaded him as scores of onlookers, including children, cheered and recorded the event on their cell phones. The Vatican reported that the priest was captured by the fighters "linked" to the Al Nusrah Front for the People in the Levant, Al Qaeda's affiliate in Syria.

The "Fides News Agency" Vatican official media outlet confirmed that Father François Murad was killed on June 23 2013 after jihadists affiliated with the Al Nusrah Front overran his monastery in Gassanieh, a town in the countryside in the northern province of Idlib in Syria.

In the video, Father Murad and two other men are seen kneeling on the ground with their hands bound behind their backs. A crowd of armed men as well as young boys watch as a bearded jihadist makes a speech. The crowd then begins to chant "Allahu Akbar" ("God is greatest"), and another bearded jihadist dressed in black takes out a knife and begins to behead one of the men. People in the crowd press close and scramble to take video. The same jihadist proceeds to behead the other two men. The heads of the murdered men are then placed on top of their corpses.

"Beheading or execution has a long history rooted in Arab, Roman and European societal and administrative setups. It is as compared to other methods used, such as crucifixion, burning at the stake, hanging, the wheel, or burying alive, the method actually represented progress and for this reason in Europe beheading was for a long time a "privilege" of the elite. Historically, the states, in the past, used it as a severe but quick punishment to remove the enemies. The Romans were the pioneer that killed thousands of their empire's opponents by beheading them in public.

John the Baptist was beheaded by **Herod**, a sub king of Roman Empire for he reproved Herod for divorcing his wife and unlawfully taking the wife of his brother. The Roman kings killed hundreds of religious saints because of their affiliations with Christianity. Similarly, after the ancient Romans, to remove the political rivals or in some cases, the so called clash of civilizations among the three big traditions Judaism, Christianity and Islam also caused heinous practicing of 'Beheading of the opponents' in England, Revolutionary France, Scotland and Arab countries respectively.

Before Islam, 'Beheading' in Arab society was happening through centuries where they slaughter and cut off the head of their enemy after killing him. The beheading of Hazrat Imam Hussain, the grandson of Muhammad and his 72 companions in the historical event of 'Karbala' in present Iraq is a crystal clear example of this Arab culture. And his 'head' was carried for miles to terrify the people. Abu Muslim Khurasani, was an Abbasid general from the Khurasani region now Afghanistan who led the Abbasid Revolution that toppled the Umayyad dynasty, was beheaded in Baghdad's castle by his own Arab master for whom he had defeated the Umayyad and installed the Abbasid dynasty in Afghanistan."------ **"Euphemism of "Beheading" from Karbala to FATA."**---

So does it happens, even in modern era; **Saudi Arabia does not tolerate public worship by adherents of religions other than Islam and systematically discriminates against its Muslim religious minorities, in particular Shia and Ismailis. The chief mufti in March called for the destruction of all churches in the Arabian Peninsula.** In 2012, authorities made arrests for expression of religious opinion, including, in February, of Hamza Kashgari, whom Malaysia extradited to the kingdom on blasphemy charges related to his fictitious Twitter dialogue with the Prophet Muhammad.

As the Sunni Muslim terrorist groups like ISIS and other Islamic jihadist echoing the same view that they won't hesitate in killing and beheading more westerners folks till the time the U.S. and its allies do not halt the airstrikes on the jihadist camps and hideouts in Iraq and Syria. It is basically becoming the battle of nerve between two formidable warring side, the Sunni-Muslims and Non-Muslims.

Britain has proved to be most affected because most of the youths (men and women) who have travelled to the Islamic countries in the middle-east and north-Africa overwhelming number of those are from Britain.

The Muslim priest or religious leaders are mostly part of sleeper cells of many jihadist terror groups like Al-Qaeda and ISIS, therefore the Muslim religious leaders have subtly taken over the responsibility of recruiting members for jihadist terror groups, they outrageously play a crucial role in hunting for mostly repressive and fanatic minded youths especially from their own Sunni-Muslim community who are feeble and easy to convince them to become jihadist and take-up arms. The Muslim priests and clerics in mainly non-Islamic countries visits societies to preach age old seventh century barbaric Islamic theology with motive to radicalize the youth men and women, falling prey to insidious religious teaching naïve as they are the men and women gets radicalize and agrees to become jihadist (holy warrior) and takes up arms in their hands and willingly travels to Arabian countries.

The objective of noxious Muslim religious or political hierarchy is not to simply radicalize youths from their own community, these inconsiderate religious clerics also prey for the youths from other non-Islamic religious or ethnic communities as well, they are always on the prowl preying to find the most vulnerable individuals from the non-Islamic community, some repressive or disgruntled non-Muslim men and women are wooed and entice to first study Islam, then they are systematically converted to Islam and radicalized and persuaded to take up arms and fight against the so-called infidels (non-Sunni Muslims).

The western countries particularly Britain and France have comprehensively failed to curb the rise of Islamic terrorism in their own backyard, the unprecedented rise of fanatics to become jihadist, and the barbaric teaching and radicalizing process has been going on and happening at alarming rate nowhere else but right under the nose of the law officers of these countries, yes, mostly in France, Britain and many more European countries as well in U.S. the process of teaching Islamic theology happens in jail of these countries itself. The savage Muslim Prison inmates (who are often religious priest and preachers) prey's for the non-Muslims prison inmates who are mostly repressive and disgruntled, it works this way, first the Muslim prison inmates will become very friendly with non-Muslims prison inmates, will than involve them in highly academic conversation and then once they become good friends and are in good terms, very cordially and cleverly and systematically the Muslim prison inmates will start the process of radicalizing the non-Muslims prison inmates, they will make them read Islamic religious literatures, will smoothly preach them how beneficial it will be for the non-Muslims to convert to Islam, so on and so forth, the Muslim prison inmates mostly succeeds in prevailing over the minds of the non-Muslims prison inmates and this is how the non-Muslims prison inmates gets radicalize and succumbs before the nefarious design of the Islamic fundamentalism, the non-Muslims prison inmates starts believing that by converting to Islam they will get closer to the divine power and by becoming jihadist (holy warrior) the doors of heaven will open for them, so this is how the terrorism and fundamentalism succeeds in many European countries. The prison cells of many European jail have for past many decades become breeding ground for jihadist and have become unofficial conversion centres of sought for non-Muslims into adopting Islam as their religion.

Women are not to be left behind, Clusters of women from mainland Europe have travelled to Syria after attending Islamic classes in mosques – from France a group of Chechen women emigrated together – but British women have tended to go alone. "The profile is very mixed across Europe. In the UK, many come from second-generation families from south Asia, because that's the biggest Muslim community in U.K. They are school leavers and a few of them are university students.

Women as well supports militants of the Islamic State (ISIS) not only with sex. The group created special women's brigade Al-Hans, named after famous ancient Arabic female poet. Sources submit that members of the all-women al-Khanssaa Brigade in Raqqa, Syria, are running brothels to satisfy the fighters' desires. They are pimping the non-Muslim women/girls out to ISIS terrorists to please the savage beasts.

The women of this brigade patrol streets to see that other women comply with Sharia laws (Islamic law). They often appear armed in public places, stopping and interrogating women, who appear on the streets unaccompanied, and check whether the men, who accompany them, are relatives, and whether women's clothes meet the requirements of the Islamic State. In addition, Al-Hans women recruit Sunni-Muslim girls for marriage with militants, as the Islamic State needs families to create a strong community of like-minded individuals. Fighters are encouraged to stay in their region, have children, and their wives should support their husbands in an effort to participate in jihad and educate Islamist ideology to children. The extremist group of the Islamic State (ISIS) actively promotes the idea of solidarity and comradeship. They create support groups, where women exchange recipes, communicate, instruct new members and give advice how to get to Syria and Iraq.

ISIS has received considerable world attention for its savage beheadings, executions of captured soldiers and men in conquered towns and villages, violence against Christians and Shiites, and the destruction of non-Sunni shrines and places of worship. But its barbarity against women has been treated as a side issue. Arab and Muslim governments, vocal on the threat ISIS poses to regional stability, have been virtually silent on ISIS's systemic degradation, abuse, and humiliation of women. To the men of ISIS, women are an inferior race, to be enjoyed for sex and be discarded, or to be sold off as slaves. From ISIS-captured territory in Syria, appeared a photograph of a line of women, covered from head to toe and tied to one another by a rope, as they were being led to a makeshift slave market. Little girls, who were going to school and playing with dolls before ISIS fighters arrived at their doorstep, were married off to men many times their age.

According to Hanafi jurist Imam al Sarakhsi (d. 1090), the Prophet Mohammed called upon jihadists to "kill the warring elders of the pagans and to keep alive their subordinates." Al Sarakhsi defines the subordinates as women and small children whom he stresses are supposed to be taken as captives, according to Islamic law. The essential problem with ISIS is that they take such teachings to the extreme. They don't just kill the "warring elders." They slaughter in the most brutal fashion imaginable every man who doesn't think like them, whether he be Yazidi, Turcoman, Christian, Shabak, Shia, or even a Sunni who doesn't buy into their extremist worldview. They behead, torture, and even crucify people, displaying the dead bodies afterwards in a barbaric fashion.

Regarding the women of their opponents, they don't merely take them captive. They massively rape them, enslave them, and force them to convert to Islam, even though the Quran clearly states "there is no compulsion in religion." As many as 1,500 Yazidis and Christians women and girls in Iraq may have been forced into sex slavery and human trafficking, the UN reports. The UN also stresses that brutal rapes have systematically been used as a weapon of war by ISIS against Yazidi, Turcoman, Christian, and Shabak community members in Iraq.

Thousands of Iraq's Yazidis community, who are driven from their homes by ISIS and trapped in the desperate siege of Mt. Sinjar, have captured the world's attention and received some relief from U.S. airstrikes and humanitarian aid. But hundreds of Yazidi women taken by ISIS and held in a secret prison where they have been raped and sold off like property are facing an equally dire fate.

Survivors who managed to escape from ISIS, said that the women held in its prison in Mosul face two fates: Those who convert to Islam are sold as brides to Islamist fighters for prices as low as US$25 and ranging up to $150. Those who do not convert face daily rape and a slow death. Accounts of the prison have come from women those who managed to cleverly hide their cellular phones, and called their relatives to describe their plight.

In the late 80s there was a commercial, "This is your brain on drugs", that gave the example of your brain as an egg, drugs as a hot frying pan and your brain being fried on drugs. Well, it turns out that it's far worse than drugs. Islam's hateful rhetoric in a woman's mind makes the 18″ drop into the heart, and infects the very soul of a woman. She begins to abandon characteristics that are inherent to her gender like: Compassion, kindness, mercy, empathy and sympathy. A woman's nature is to nurture…that is, until Islam beats a woman senseless. Islam's dictates fester in a man till acted out against women…and women see little to no worth in themselves. And, apparently, when a woman is subjected to this misogynistic creed long enough…she joins the dark side.

The world is getting increasingly destabilize and uncertain, since the year 2012 it gives us sense of feeling, like an unofficial 3rd world war has already started, with almost the whole world at loggerhead, the Hawkish Russian leader President/dictator Vladimir Putin perilously rubbing shoulder the wrong way with peer western power, the Russians have adopted a very aggressive policy with regards to its immediate neighbour countries, Russia trying its best to capture by force the power to rule and dominate the social, economic and political policies of prominent eastern-European countries who share their borders with Russia, Russia attacked Georgia than systematically destabilize a thriving Ukraine, Russia demolished the peace of the Ukrainians by breaking up the country. Equally troublesome is another large and powerful country China, after gaining huge economic prosperity, the Chinese have become more aggressive and pragmatic, the Chinese are not hesitating in dominating its neighbours, China is causing immense trouble to its neighbours and has enormous territorial dispute with India, Vietnam, Japan etc, the ebullient Islamic army is cohesively moving on aggressive path and challenging the mighty and powerful nations, all these adds up to immense pain to we humans, selfish motives and actions of power-hungry men that's what is destabilizing the world's ecology and economies.

We are living in a chaotic world, once successful countries that were land of opportunities, where there was considerable peace and prosperity, such countries like, Iraq, Libya, Syria, Egypt, Yemen, Somalia and Tunisia, now all these countries have become failed state, millions of its citizens are hard pressed as they have lost their livelihood and are displaced either living in refugee camps under most sordid living conditions, worse still their children face bleak future prospects. But, there is also another country which as well was once a power house of eastern Europe, I'm talking about Ukraine which was thriving economic centre famous for its black soil land which makes Ukraine arguably the best fertile land for agriculture in the world, also Ukraine skilled work force is famous for supplying to the world the most advanced Hi-Tech industrial machinery, unfortunately Ukraine is plunged into most horrific political crisis with its powerful neighbour Russia's oppressive regime is brutally suppressing Ukraine.

Soviet union may have collapse the so-called cold war between Russian and U.S and its European allies may have been over, but, Russia under the leadership of audacious president Mr Vladimir Putin does not want to play second fiddle to the dominance of the U.S. and it crony, Russians are trying to carve a niche for themselves as they want to prove their prowess and become an equally dominating player on the global political scene. Hence planned strategy is "not behind curve but stay ahead of curve" the belligerent Russian president Putin is not scared to rub shoulders the wrong way with the western countries political power houses.

Western countries though are rallying behind Ukraine and rendering their support, led by U.S. and west-European nations like Britain, France And Germany are strongly backing Ukraine's political leadership in their fight to combat suppressive Russian forces, the western countries imposed sanctions on Russia for its savage and disruptive policy role of disturbing internal peace in Ukraine by directly indulging in causing division of Ukraine. The western nations impose punitive economic sanctions against Russia, an act of punishing Russia for it disruptive political policies of threatening its east-European neighbouring nations, however unperturbed Russian president retaliated by imposing counter sanctions against European Union nations. Not just that, the Russian president also throwing daring challenge and threatens the western countries that if they take any stringent measures to defend or to favour Ukraine, and if western countries impose any more harsh economic sanctions against Russia, that will be construed as provocative and hence Russia may retaliate fire with fire, Russia is threatening western countries that it may put a ban on European airlines from using the Russian airstrip, that means Russia will not allow the European and American airplanes to fly over Russia air space, a move that will prove devastatingly harmful economically for the west-European and U.S. aviation industry, also one must not forget that Russia is the biggest supplier of oil & gas to European countries, hence the western European countries hands are tied as they are so overwhelmingly dependent on Russian oil & gas, thus they have very little room to manoeuvre as far as them dealing with, ever so, vigorous and volatile leader like Russian president Putin.

It is also alleged, however there have been allegations and counter allegation over who bombed or blasted the Malaysian Airline airplane "MH17" that was ferociously blasted allegedly by the Russian backed and supported Ukrainian separatist rebels. Whosoever may have done it but such crimes committed, like the one that of blasting the airplane MH17, puts humanity to shame.

The policies and politics of sanctions and imposing sanctions is very peculiar and precarious. The imposition of economic and diplomatic, military arms and weapons sanctions, means, when a group of countries unite and connive and decides on imposition of sanctions on a country whose political leadership or regime is perceived by group of countries to be dictatorial, corrupt, oppressive or rogue regime which are declared outlawed and oppressive regime, so, when sanctions are impose, the economic and trade embargo are the most common among the list of sanctions that are imposed on such alleged rogue countries, well, the records speaks for themselves, the history of imposing sanctions in past or present, there is a long list of countries who have at some point in time in the past or some in the present have experienced or are experiencing the harshness of sanctions which are imposed on them, but, as the record speaks for themselves that the sanctions have always failed to have desire impact and failed to garner desire results, the sanctions never have or doesn't really harm the political and religious hierarchy, for example, Iraq was under sanction for 13 years under Saddam's regime, but, evidently it proved futile because the dictator Saddam and his sons and their cronies were unharmed as they vividly rejoiced every moment of their life till they were dislodge from power by the American arm forces, same is the story of North-Korean dictator, and many more dictators who have rejoiced and lived life king-size despite stiff economic and diplomatic sanctions, also to point out countries like Iran and Syria to name a few from the long list of countries have so vehemently survived stiff economic and diplomatic sanctions imposed against them.

But, the sanctions does have grave and significant impact on common-men, the sanction when impose on a country does have unintended consequences but on civilian population, which are very grim. When the country is put under sanctions it may not at all harm the political and religious leaderships but the common-people of the country under sanctions have to suffer extreme pain, because their livelihood is severely impacted, their monthly earnings take a hit hence it becomes extremely difficult for the people to meet ends.

When there is financial instability and people of a country are apprehensive about their future which looks bleak, that's when under duress and disgust some people snap their patience, their agony compels them to make agonizing choices, hence some of them under pressure and compulsions turns rogue individuals as they without any bit of hesitation takes plunge into intimate world, adopts sleazy professions like women and girls are most likely to become prostitutes or drug peddlers, child marriages forced marriages becomes a norm, men's often becomes human traffickers, pimps, criminals or terrorist. So, one problem creates many more problems, all this adds to the misery and harms the peace and unity and makes world more unsafe.

So, the intellectual class, political and social scientist should find some better way of dealing with the so-called outlawed oppressive regimes that at times devastates the world.

Who does it and why? How things are manipulated? The best effective strategy and policy the political class and religious hierarchy have is to polarize their political constituency and seriously brainwash their naïve followers. It is a tried and tested formula which has worked so wonderfully well ever since recorded history of we humans, and, how to do it? Well, it is ever so simple, all they have to do is to systematically radicalize the civil society, which is also called divide and rule policy. We the people for generations have been bitterly divided among ourselves on racial ground or on different religious beliefs.

A critical part of radicalization is often in the way the message is socialized, becoming a central part of everyday conversation outside of the rallying hall. For socialization to work best, this conversation should be contained, with any contrary messages being kept at bay. Where possible, the people will be isolated to insulate them from external dissuasion. Where this is not possible, inoculation may be used to help them ward off other views. Groupthink and other social means of ensuring conformance may also be used to keep people on track. When the transgression leads to some people seeking revenge then they may seek to organize in some way, recruiting and converting others to the cause.

The call to arms goes through many channels, typically targeting groups where members may already feel the sense of injustice, such as minority religions, the unemployed, low-status women and so on. Other vulnerable people may well also be targeted. Communication may include preaching, emails posters, one-to-one calls and so on. While these do not radicalize alone, they often take the first step in communicating urgency or outrage. Later, the volume and intensity of messages create enough tension to trigger action.

Initial communication may be subtle and seemingly about other subjects. Religions can be like this, first creating a desirable place, selling friendship and salvation before radical action. Sooner or later, the subject of discussion turns to the basic transgression, including the mistreatment or immorality and the consequent sense of outrage. This creates anger and a desire for action. A key part of the message is to demonize the other side, objectifying the people as subhuman, using amplification, negative stereotypes and simplified schema. In doing so, the argument is polarized. By showing that the other side is so extreme, the simple conclusion is reached that extreme action is the only possible route forward. The arguments used may well be full of fallacies but the passion and underlying messages are clear.

Mistreatments today such as rape and child abuse are also extreme transgressions that effectively radicalize those who would severely punish the perpetrators. Many of us who think we would never be radicalized still hold extreme views on such topics. The process of radicalization often starts with some form of transgression by the other side, breaking rules that the person's side holds as very important. A common transgressing action is mistreatment, typically by the authorities or military personnel using methods that cause extreme physical pain or mental distress. The mistreatment may be of the person who hence becomes radicalized, but often it is other people who are lionized as heroes or martyrs. Mistreatment can be historical and reasons for radicalization can go back generations. Past wars, massacres, persecutions and so on can fester for hundreds of years.

"If political channels are open, so everyone can participate equally in the process, the chances of a radical group having to resort to violence in order to be heard are lower," One condition that can lead to the making of a terrorist is the lack of political means to have complaints heard and addressed. Such barriers are common even in democracies, where the suspicion that one's views are being ignored can lead to political violence. "However, if such channels limit who can participate, then those who are excluded from the process will feel great humiliation, which triggers deep emotions such as anger and hate—especially if they are rejected as a result of their group identity."

There are a lot of different ways in which people use the term. People use it very broadly to refer to the process of embracing ideas that are outside of widely accepted religious or political spectrum. So they use it to refer to, for example, Muslims who believe in the restoration of the caliphate. People have used it to talk about Tea Party politicians who have argued that private businesses should be allowed to discriminate. But in the wake of 9/11, the term has been used narrowly to mean the process that leads people — particularly Muslims — to embrace violence as a means for achieving political or social change.

One way to assess the trajectory of a given group is to first understand why its members are together—what their core issues and concerns are. How and to whom have they communicated their issues and complaints, and how have the issues been received? Have they been acknowledged and perhaps addressed? For example, have these groups petitioned the government or marched in public events? And what have the government and the public done as a result of such activities?

As an example, the tragedy in Norway. On July 22, 2011, Anders Behring Breivik, disguised as a police officer, opened fire on participants of a youth event sponsored by the ruling Norwegian Labour Party. Breivik killed 69 people. He was also responsible for a car-bomb explosion in Oslo earlier the same day, which killed eight people and wounded several others. Indeed, Breivik did feel that way, and on the day of the attacks, he posted a 1,518-page manifesto, "2083—A European Declaration of Independence," outlining his militant anti-immigration and anti-Islam far-right ideology. But he had never hidden his views. He had been expressing them for years on Internet forums. When you look at Norway in terms of its socioeconomic and political systems, it is the best place in the world. It has a very high quality-of-life index and is very democratic. And yet we have the tragic incident that happened—a 'lone-wolf' terrorist incident. Although this type of incident is nearly impossible to predict, there were conditions before the event that could have been used to anticipate the potential for violence. For example, would it have been possible to sense that some people in Norway felt that their country was losing its identity because of too many immigrants? Could some have felt a sense of invasion?

I think it's really important to recognize that radicalization as most people talk about it has two components. One is speech and religious activity that's protected by the Constitution. The other component is criminal activity such as preparing for a violent act or raising money for a terrorist organization. That end of the spectrum is worrisome.

The existence of such vulnerable people, coupled with the growth of groups that think they cannot engage in conventional societal and political processes, are the first conditions society must be aware of when attempting to identify a possibly violent or hate-driven group. Much like cults, terrorist groups encourage or intimidate people to abandon their families and adopt the terrorist organization as their new family. The organization can use its family-like roles and relationships to focus a great amount of peer pressure on its members, compelling them to do acts of terrorism. "Radical groups are not shy about stating their goals, claims, and objectives," A high rate of unemployment is also a condition for creating hate groups and political violence. "I am concerned about the large numbers of unemployed recent college graduates with significant student loan debt in many countries."

Chapter 6

I remember that day 11-sept-2001 (9/11) sitting in my house in Mumbai, it was evening time the dusk was above to fall, as per my routine affair, I switched on my TV set and tuned it on the news channel to catch up with the latest news, the horror struck me, when every news channels in India all national and international news channels broke the horrific news of the attack on America's iconic New-York city's Twin Towers and few other places in U.S. as well which were attacked by the Islamist jihadist terrorists, led by group called Al-Qaeda which apparently was headed by none other than "Osama Bin laden," "**America Under Attack**" was the headline news on every channels I could see, it was a rude shock obviously not just for my family and me but for the whole world, devastated emotionally by seeing the images that were being broadcast on every news channels the world over.

Like newton's theory every action has an equal reactions, hence on the expected lines, the 9/11 attack was not an attack on an ordinary third world country that would just keep its mouth shut and take the blow rendered by the terrorists on their chin.

The outcry of spontaneous passion, shell shocked American citizens and U.S. political leadership flabbergast, nervous reaction witnessed from wall-street to high-streets, traders and merchants and baffled political class, the onus was again on the then U.S. president "George W Bush" to take initiatives of dealing with gruesome and heinous crime perpetrated against the mighty "United states of America," the 9/11 refreshed for many Americans the memory of "12/7," here I'm referring to the 20th century brutal Pearl Harbour attack that had occurred on the U.S. soil on "December-7-1941, by the Japanese's Naval forces. The Japanese attack inflicted on Pearl Harbour also became a catalyst for U.S. to directly enter the World-War II fight.

The heinous terror incident of 9/11 became a catalyst for the non-Islamist religions and ideologies to wage war against their common formidable enemy "Islam."

In disgust and anguish the U.S. president "George W Bush" put up a spirited brave front as he as the commander in chief of U.S. army forces assured citizens of his beleaguered country post 9/11 attack, Mr Bush with his determined rhetoric tried to bolster the confidence of people by assuring people of America and the world that he would take a lead and wage war on terror and will leave no stone unturned to decimate the terrorist infrastructures and eliminate the terrorism. He made that famous declaration "**America is at war against terrorist and terrorism,**" Vowing before people of his nation and the world that he would eradicate terrorism from the world's map.

Not only Mr Bush the president of U.S. but every colleague of his from White-house started a major PR exercise to try to cobble up support for their resolve in destroying the terror network around the world. The world political leaders expressing their grief and showing their solidarity pledged support to America and agreed to help U.S. president in his endeavour to extinguish the terrorist from the map of the world.

The sceptics and critics of Mr George W Bush however preferred to remain silence and watch the proceedings from distance as they wanted to see how the move initiated by U.S. president on his war on terror will work, the sceptics strategy was to wait and watch and see how things unravel, before they start talking and commenting if at all any kind or type of failure or what its end consequences will be.

Unperturbed and undeterred US president Mr Bush without bothering about his critics, he moved on along with his friends and allies and launched aggressive, categorical and emphatic "**War on terror,**" American arm forces towards the end of the year 2001 launched emphatic attack on the terrorist camp inside

Afghanistan which was the principle base of Al-Qaeda at that time also it is allege that "Bin Laden" the founder of Al-Qaeda use to stay in Afghanistan at that time.

With regards to president "George W Bush" plan and policy of war on terror, at the very beginning of the war on terror, there were lots of optimist including I myself who believed that Mr Bush's intentions are humble and his inspired war on terror will yield desired result, and the terror and terrorists will be wiped out and this world will become a better and safe place to live in. but, however in another camp there were overt and sly sceptics and pessimist who firmly were of the opinion that the manner in which Mr Bush is pursuing his plan policies vis a vis war on terror will prove to be a futile exercise and will have devastating and disastrous consequence and world will become a more unsafe place to live in.

The determined American army in the war on terror managed to topple the Iraqi dictator Saddam, and also dismissed the fundamentalist Taliban government in Afghanistan. Saddam and his sons met their fate, Saddam's two sons were killed, while Saddam himself was trail in court of justice and he was hanged to death, the allege master conspirator of 9/11, the founder and head of Al-Qaeda terrorist group Osama Bin laden too was captured and killed.

But, did the terrorists perish or terrorism extinct from the world, has this world become a safe place to live in? The answer is an **emphatic "NO,"** not at all in fact as a result of war on terror, the terrorism has become even more dreaded and vigorous. The segmented and Fragmented Sunni-Muslim groups have become more united then they were ever before and the new generation as well as the old generations people who follow Sunni Islam have become or are becoming more and more radicalized and more determined to fight for the cause of Islam, therefore becoming jihadist whom others perceives as terrorist.

In many major cities around the world like "Mumbai, Bali, Nairobi, Madrid, London etc are the cities which have in the aftermath of the war on terror have come under unsparing terror attack ruthlessly carried out by the various factions Islamist jihadist groups.

The war on terror has proved to be an inconclusive and painful, more so extraordinarily expensive futile exercise. Nearly trillion U.S. Dollars have been spent as the cost of war on terror and the spending of unprecedented amount of money is still continuing as part of the policy to curb and eliminate terrorism, millions of people belonging to almost every religion and beliefs have lost their lives, and many thousands have lost their limbs and severely wounded other parts of their body.

Just to put things in perspective and to describe infamous War on Terror in few words; it's a Trillion Dollar blood-soaked blunder.

Famous Pakistani former cricketer and politician Imran khan a vocal critic and bitter opponent of the U.S. and its allies policy of hitting at allege terrorist targets and bases inside Pakistan, has been saying that the U.S. military policy of striking at terrorist hideouts and camps inside Pakistan and Afghanistan by flying Drone (unmanned combat aerial aircraft), the drone strikes often misses its desire targets and kills innocent civilians, Imran Khan, whose Tehreek-e-Insaf party runs the "Khyber Pakhtunkhwa" provincial government, demands that federal officials to take a firmer stance to force the US to end drone attacks and block NATO supplies across the country. Imran views that such Misfiring of targets and killing of civilians, the casualties and fatality of innocent people are further alienating the Muslims and driving them further away from the western countries and Non-Islamic people and are becoming more radicalise and hence the war on terror is only increasing the resolve of resenting Muslims to become jihadist and fight against the Americans and other western countries whom fundamentalist Muslims perceives as infidels.

The apprehension and concern raised initially by the critics of the 43rd president of United States "Mr George W Bush" have proved to be correct, the war on terror that started in 2001 in the aftermath of the terror attack on US has proved and is proving to be an unending saga, the Islamic terror has become more intense than it ever was. Maybe, Mr Bush may have taken the lead in waging the war on terror in right earnest, we must not doubt Mr Bush efforts, maybe Mr Bush's intentions were humble, or did he and his crony had any sly motives, well these are loaded questions and lingering doubts that will forever be debated and discussed, but one thing is for sure that the war on terror has proved to be lengthy indecisive, meaningless and directionless.

Western countries heads of states (presidents & prime ministers) strongly worded rhetoric like we'll "degrade and destroy" the terrorist network and eliminate terrorism, these kind of motivational language that they speak while addressing the press and their citizens, these heads of states by speaking such strong language can score political points and gain support and popularity in opinion polls succeed in boosting their personal image, but they will not be able to defeat the terrorist "**Period.**"

You can win wars and battles by firing bullets and missiles and by throwing bombs from fighter Aircrafts, but, the Islamic jihadist ideological base is firm and spread far and wide, simply by killing the "Osama's, Saddam's, Gaddafi's" of the world or destroying Ottoman Empire, the secularist can't defeat the fanaticism of Islamic jihadist ideology, those people who follow the principles of jihad (Islamic holy war) have very stiff and rigid mind-sets, the jihadists can be defeated in the battle fields, but the jihadists (Islamic holy warriors) intent and determination has and will always remain that of defiant and confrontationist. The Islamic jihadist are willing to die for their religion without any regrets, Kill few jihadists --- so what -- but so many more jihadist will take birth, the firing bullets and missiles will get over but not the jihadists.

So, what is the best and better way to deal and to neutralize the jihadist? The best way to defeat the jihadist philosophy and ideology, Not by aggression, but by taking bold initiatives and pragmatic social approach, which will be cost effective and economical also ecologically friendly way, which in my thinking could solve at least the Islamic terror issues once and for all, that is: make no mistake, the innocent Islamic factions should not be victimised, rightly distinguish appropriate faction of Islam (Sunni-Islam) that has for generations been practising the barbaric Islamic laws, **that particular faction should be socially boycotted in every possible way treat those fanatics Muslim factions in total like a social pariah,** not to relent until such time that they relinquish their generations old Islamic theology and ideologies and shed outdated philosophy. **This is the only way to win "war on terror," not by bullets.**

America's mantra after the end of 1st world war has been: "**we are the leader, we'll lead, you follow us**; US believes as it is the only super power nation and it has economic and military supremacy hence U.S. because of its capability wants to play significant and decisive role in every worldly matters, U.S. wants to dominate every country's domestic and foreign policies, OK, but what has the U.S. achieved for itself over the past many years and decades by playing such dominant role.

When a person/persons have lots of money and power he/she becomes insane, when a person is impecunious he/she becomes mad, so, what it means is that the more powerful you are the equal is your vulnerability, both, the rich and the poorest are equally insecure. The more you try to play a dominant role the more you will be criticised for your big brotherly attitudes. And, America being the world's largest economy and a land of opportunities, most of the world's richest people live in U.S., so, considering itself mighty and powerful the Americans feels that it is there social and moral responsibility to play a lot bigger role in international political and social affairs. And so is the U.S. desirously doing it, directly or indirectly, overtly or discreetly, American interference is visible almost in every parts of the world, but, how beneficial has it prove for America to be so bothered and concerned about others internal and external matters.

America's foreign policies has always been proved a doom, some of the failures are worth highlighting, in the mid-1930s during Japanese aggression against China, when China and Japan were involved in bitter and bloody tussles, US intervene in the internal matters between China and Japan, U.S. sided with the secular Chinese regime and opposed Japan's aggression and atrocities against Chinese, the US move infuriated Japan to such an extent, as a result of which, Japan retaliated by blasting the American territory of pearl harbour, Japan intention to blast pearl harbour was to contain and stop US from protecting the Asian nations that Japan wanted to capture and rule, hugely devastated and shocked the United states of America under duress and compulsion had to enter the ongoing world war at that time in the early 1940s.

After the 2nd world war, resentful civil war broke out in Korea between two distinctly different political ideologies, the Korean civil war was between communist and secular liberal forces, here again US had to intervene, obviously US sided with the secular liberal faction inside Korea, the intensely fought battle in Korea between US backed secular forces and China backed communist forces, the war lasted nearly 3 years, the end result, ultimately Korea was divided in communist ruled North-Korea and secularist ruled South-Korea, and ever since the North-Korea has become a staunch enemy of US, north Korean regime spares no opportunity to harm US, likewise US intervention in the

Vietnam civil war in the 1960s as well proved to be a big fiasco, many US soldiers lost their lives and many more returned back to US with un-healable injuries, similarly U.S. wars to establish secular democracy in countries like Afghanistan and Iraq as well proved nothing but chaotic, US war in Afghanistan and Iraq has shattered the peace of almost half the world's population.

These are just few examples to prove that how wrong and futile has been America's overseas adventures, U.S. will be better advice to save its own democracy and not to interfere in overseas matter at least not unilaterally.

America has its own share of woes for which it's political and business leadership is spending less time in dealing with. Internally in U.S. as well there is socio-economic inequality, racial and religious tensions, worse still the **notorious Gun violence** which has become a menace and has killed thousands of people over past many decades. Instead of addressing there domestic issues which are of such serious significance and not to ignore US is also suffering from major ecological crisis as well, the flash floods, hurricane, droughts that outrageously keeps occurring on recurring basis in different regions of United-States, my sincere advice to American political leadership would be that please don't bother much about outside world, you have a lots of pending work to be done in your own backyard, particularly dealing with those repressive psychopaths who are resorting to **Gun violence** and randomly killing innocent people in public places.

In U.S.A between 2002 and 2014 just a couple of hundred citizens were killed by the Terrorists, -- but, Tens of Thousands of innocent U.S citizens killed in Gun Violence, also during this period other social problems and domestic violence increased as well. U.S. politicians need to stop playing role of mediator in solving other countries internal and external problems, instead they concentrate more and spend more time on solving their own domestic problems. ---- Muslims will sort out Islamic problems, --- Persians and Arabs will sort out Arabian problems, ----- if there is crisis in Europe than the French, Germans and Russians will sit together and negotiate solution, if there is dispute in Far-east Asia between Koreans, Chinese and Japanese, better be left for the Chinese and Japanese to sort out their dispute, but, America should simply stay out of all dispute talks, let others sort out and resolve their own problems in their own way.

Reacting sharply to the gruesome murder of two American journalist "James Foley and Steven Sotloff " by ISIS terrorist, the US Vice President Joseph Biden denounced the beheading of Sotloff in a speech at a naval shipyard in

New Hampshire, declaring that US military forces would pursue ISIS to "the gates of hell." Yes, your brave army will, indeed, Mr Vice-President Biden we appreciate your determined courageous speech and effort. But just a point to be noted here is, that, ISIS is not an incomprehensible emanation of Satanic evil, as portrayed by the Obama administration and the American media. It is a product of the policies of the US government over a protracted period of time. US administrations have sought to build up the most reactionary and backward Islamic fundamentalist forces in the Middle East for many decades. Throughout the Cold War, Washington mobilized them against secular nationalist leaders viewed either as potential allies of the Soviet Union or as direct threats to the profits and property of American and European corporations.

The CIA financed and mobilized right-wing Iranian Islamists in support of the 1953 coup that ousted the liberal government of Mohammed Mossadegh, which had nationalized the largely British-owned oil industry. The US cultivated similar forces in Egypt, including the Muslim Brotherhood, to undermine the regime of Colonel Gamal Abdel Nasser, who nationalized the Suez Canal and sought military aid from the Soviet Union. In 1977, the CIA backed the coup in Pakistan carried out by Muhammad Zia-ul-Haq, who established a martial law regime based on Islamist fundamentalism that lasted until his death in 1988.

The security anchor of American policy in the Persian Gulf region, particularly after the 1979 revolution that overthrew the Shah of Iran, was an alliance with the monarchy in Saudi Arabia, which has long promoted the most reactionary forms of Islamic fundamentalism as an ideological bulwark for its parasitic rule. The state of Israel pursued a similar policy, promoting the Muslim Brotherhood affiliate in the occupied Palestinian territories as a rival to undermine the Palestine Liberation Organization of Yasser Arafat, which it viewed as the main enemy. Out of this effort would emerge Hamas and Islamic Jihad.

The inhumanity of the Saudi regime frequently recently in order to demonstrate the incredible hypocrisy of U.S. foreign policy. While America's phony politicians and useless mainstream media will often hype anti-Christian bigotry and humanitarian issues when it suits the status quo message, **the true driver of U.S. foreign policy can be summarized with two words: CORPORATE PROFITS.**

To better understand from different angle and to get better perspective about the wars and terrorism, There is other side as well, strife torn and war ravaged as well as terrorism marred countries also provides excellent business opportunity for arms and ammunition industry, globally weapons arms and ammunition and other military hardware and software annual business according to some estimate is valued over One Trillion US-Dollar, hence the demand for weapons and ammunition is huge and it increases further if their persist civil unrest and bickering between governments or religious communities escalates and transform into full blown conflict.

Such incidents and events opens up windows of opportunities for the companies that manufactures and trades in arms and weapons, world's prominent countries which are the biggest arms manufacturers and exporters are "United States, Russia, France, China and Britain," all these countries are fierce rivals of each other and intensely compete against each other to gain defence supply contracts particularly from developing and third world nations, and subtly deals with outlawed rebels and terrorists groups.

The weapons and ammunition purchase and procurement procedures of any country is always a highly sensitive matter, the decision making of purchasing weapons involves many people from diverse field, there is always differences among politicians and government officials for what kind and types of arms will be most suitable for their country's defence force, that's when the power brokers (wheeler/dealer' the liaise) and arms dealers steps in to woo and convince the politician and military officials as in what would be most appropriate weapons to purchase, these astute and influential power brokers and arms dealers/agents throws exciting and tempting offers, lots of money changes hands from under the table, it is also allege and at times seen on some TV news channels in sting operation that the power brokers and the agents of the arms manufacturer serves best of "wine' women and wealth" to the voracious politician and government officials of the country to whom they have to sell their weapons. Because there is too much money involve, that's why, there is always lots of corruption involve as well from both sides in the purchase/sell of arms and ammunitions, the buyer of weapons is corrupt and greedy so is the seller and dealers.

The **arms industry** is a global business that manufactures weapons and military technology and equipment. It consists of commercial **industry** involved in research, development, production, and the service of military material, equipment, and facilities. Arms producing companies, also referred to as defence contractors or military industry, produce arms mainly for the armed forces of states. Departments of government also operate in the arms industry, buying and selling weapons, munitions and other military items.

Contracts to supply a given country's military are awarded by the government, making arms contracts of substantial political importance. The link between politics and the arms trade can result in the development of what once former U.S. President Dwight D Eisenhower described as a **military-industrial congressional complex**, where the armed forces, commerce, and politics become closely linked. The European defence procurement is more or less analogous to the U.S. military-industrial complex. Various corporations, some publicly held, others private, bid for these contracts, which are often worth many billions of dollars. Sometimes, such as the contract for the new joint strike fighter, a competitive tendering process takes place, where the decision is made on the merits of the design submitted by the companies involved. Other times, no bidding or competition takes place.

The modern arms industry emerged in the second half of the nineteenth century as a product of the creation and expansion of the first large military-industrial companies. As smaller countries (and even newly industrializing countries like Russia and Japan) could no longer produce cutting-edge military equipment with their indigenous resources and capacity, they increasingly began to contract the manufacture of military equipment, such as battleships, artillery pieces and rifles to foreign firms.

Predictably, this innovation involves the global arms market, which by all accounts is the source of more bribes than any other sector. And although most actors in the global arms trade have abandoned briefcases of unmarked, non-consecutive bills for the relative security of Foreign Sales Corporations and shell companies, corruption watchdogs are rarely more than a few steps behind – nipping at their perfidious heels. Thus the real trophy for crooked public officials and their private sector counterparts is not finding extra-legal ways to hide corrupt transactions, but changing the law to make existing practices legal. Enter the Holy Grail of graft – "defence offsets." Offsets are incentive contracts that defence manufacturers sign with procuring governments to facilitate weapons sales. They usually take the form of substantial investments in the importing country's indigenous defence industry or some politically important commercial sector.

In addition to being opaque and unregulated, offsets also perform many of the same functions as bribes: they allow competing firms to sweeten their bids outside the ordinary channels of price and quality-competition, and offsets provide officials in the procuring country with opportunities to direct benefits to their domestic political allies. Lastly, like an unpaid bribe, suing a defence firm for non-fulfilment of an offset is (quite literally) unheard of.

So, arms are traded both legally and illegally, those who purchase arms illegally are mostly the terrorist or outlawed rebel private army or insurgent forces, hence their exist a huge illegal arms market and big amount of money is made by the traders and manufacturers of weapons, as it serves purpose of many peoples, hence, avaricious individuals as well as corrupt governments of many countries deliberately orchestrate social tensions between various different religions, ethnic minority and majority communities of the country, as well as between different political ideologies like the liberal democrats and extreme socialist and communist, other reasons that becomes potential cause of instability and turmoil resulting in conflicts is when a country is marred with high level of corruption and hyperinflation. Unemployment and rising cost of living could damage the peace and tranquillity of the affected country, thereby provides opportunity for astute Opportunistic or the Fundamentalist forces to exploit the disgruntled elements from within the society, tempt them with lucrative deals and offers and compel them into becoming miscreants, for example: many jobless and underemployed youths (young men and women) in countries like Yemen, Pakistan, Afghanistan etc; have adopted corrupt and inhuman practice, becoming professional jihadist (Islamic holy warrior), terrorist, drug trafficker or prostitutes, simply because of poverty and allegedly because of very high degree of corruption in the political system of their country.

It has been observed that differences between religious of political ideologies leads to conflict between either the countries or it gives rise to rebellion within ranks and file resulting in insurgency which escalates into either low scale protracted war or full blown battle between conflicting groups with each of the warring factions having their own selfish motives and interests, and the more there is conflict and confrontations the more there will be demand for weapons of all types.

So, interesting as it is, there's need for us to dwell a little more to understand the reasons behind brutal crimes and wars.

Let us understand a little more; **Are wars and conflicts orchestrated for commercial purpose?**

Article title, "The Suicide of Europe," stated: "Muslims are rioting in Afghanistan because US interrogators at Guantanamo Bay flushed copies of the Koran down the toilet.

How do the rioters know this?
It was reported in Newsweek, a publication owned by the family of Eugene Meyer, a past Director of the War Finance Board (WW1), Governor of the Federal Reserve and President of the World Bank.
Nothing appears in the mass media without an ulterior purpose. The Illuminati is promoting a clash of "civilizations" between Islam and the US.
In the present run-up to World War Three, it is worth asking if this sinister cabal also orchestrated World War Two, which saw the genocide of 70 million human beings.
Was the World-war 2 orchestrated? The headquarters of the "Communist-Capitalist International" was in the City of London. The Bank of England network financed the Nazi war machine just as it financed the Bolshevik revolution. The bankers orchestrated the World War Two to concentrate wealth in their hands, destroy the great nation states of Europe and wipe out the cream of the new generation. For example, the Soviets slaughtered 15,000 Polish officers in the Katyn forest even though the Poles could have helped resist the Nazis.

Was Canaris Illuminati or an illuminati dupe? Apparently he wanted to overthrow Hitler and end the war early, but the Allies insisted on "unconditional surrender," example maximum slaughter. Thus the German army had no choice but to fight to the end. I don't see Second World War as "the good war." It was fabricated to further degrade and demoralize humanity; both sides of unspeakable atrocities."----- **"(Henry Makow)**.....

Have a listen to another theory in brief: "Without the capital provided by Wall Street, there would have been no Hitler and no WW2. In his book *'Wall Street and the Rise of Hitler'* Professor Anthony G Sutton writes that "General Motors, Ford, General Electric, DuPont," and other "U.S. companies intimately involved with the development of Nazi Germany were ... controlled by the Wall Street banks," such as "the J.P. Morgan firm, the Rockefeller Chase Bank and to a lesser extent the Warburg Manhattan bank."

Standard Oil provided a steady supply of oil throughout the war. The oil was shipped to Spain then piped through Nazi-controlled France into Germany. General Motors and Ford provided 90 % of Nazi armoured trucks. IBM produced the Hollerith machines that helped SS Officers manage the roundup of dissidents for concentration camps.

The German Army had the massive British expeditionary force at their mercy at Dunkirk in May 1940 but, on Hitler's orders, held back for three days, thereby allowing 338,000 British and French troops to escape. The German generals, waiting approval to launch a full-scale assault, were left scratching their heads. This military blunder is inexplicable by conventional standards. Why did Hitler hold back? The Illuminati wanted WW2 to be a long and bloody conflict - but one Germany would lose. The destruction of the British Army would have given the Nazis an almost unassailable advantage in the war, so Hitler had to let them escape.

Hitler was a Trojan horse designed to destroy Germany's national, cultural and racial pretensions, therefore integrating the country into a world government. This is why, instead of executing a sensible strategy to defeat the Allies, he launched a suicidal invasion of the USSR." ----**"Eight sign Illuminati orchestrated WW2."**……..

"The Israeli "security publication," DEBKA, a key part of their "war through deception" campaign against the world, has now made it inexorably clear, Israel is putting into motion their "final solution," a campaign to pit nation against nation.
The result, the planet a smouldering ruin, Israel ruling over the ashes and mass graves, is a foregone conclusion, at least to Netanyahu and his worldwide terrorist   network.

DEBKA openly admits plans to move Israeli troops into Syria and Iraq, to "con" Turkey, Jordan and the Arab and Gulf States into a war intended to, not just destroy Iran and Pakistan but China and Russia as well, pitting them against NATO in the fatal Armageddon they and their followers believe will ensure Satan's dominion over man.

The plans are clear, an invasion of Syria, splitting the Kurdish region of Iraq off, into an Israeli controlled military bastion for an invasion of Iran. What isn't being said, however, is that, in order to push the United States back to war after a decade of military and economic disasters, assassinations, false flag terror and a campaign of counterfeit WMD intelligence is planned.

The proposed moves, as outlined below and confirmed through DEBKA, would require the United States to return to "Bush era unilateralism," moves unlikely if President Obama, Secretaries Kerry and Hagel and JCOS Chief, General Martin Dempsey were still alive, despite wild conspiratorial claims." ----- **"Caught Israel orchestrating World War."**......

Chapter 7

Though I have sincere regards for politicians and I personally love politics, many politicians are and have been my ideal and I've in my life gained lots of inspiration from their inspiring speeches, I don't want to disparage politics and politicians, but, in a lighter mood, I would like to comment, that: the Politicians as well the Religious hierarchy of various religions are like **Two Headed Snakes**. When we see the movement of Political or Religious Honchos, We never know or it is always difficult to make out seeing them whether if they are moving up or down the ladder.

No I don't meant to disregard or disrespect the political or religious leaders but these classes have always had and have outrageous double standards, they don't practice what they preach, they talk something and do something else, they are notorious in breaking promises.

There has always been deep and comprehensive nexus between "Politics, Religion and Terrorist," religion can't survive without politics and politician can't survive without the support of religious hierarchy, and terrorist and terrorism is inspired and motivated by insular religious belief, hence, terrorist can't survive without support from religious hierarchy and political patronage.

Both political leadership and religious hierarchy are cunning in their manoeuvres and sly in their motives, the classic examples of political leaders double standard is worth discussing.

In the year 2014, in the Ukrainian political turmoil, when Ukraine democratic government was facing internal insurgency, when some pro-Russian and anti-government groups in some cities in southern and eastern part of Ukraine had taken to the street demonstrating in the aftermath of Euromaidan movement and 2014 Ukraine Revolution, when the demonstration turned into full blown civil war as the pro-Russian protestors turned rebel insurgent and started demanding freedom from central Ukraine government in the eastern parts of Ukraine. The western-European and the U.S. openly supporting and siding with the Ukrainian government, and alleging that Vladimir Putin Russian government administration is fomenting trouble inside Ukraine by providing profound material and monetary support to the rebel insurgent inside Ukraine. The western countries like U.S. and western European nations levelling charges and allegation against Russian president Putin for disturbing peace in democratic Ukraine they impose strict economic sanction against Russia. Well maybe the western countries did the right thing by imposing sanction on Russia for its alleged role in provoking and abating the rebel forces in Ukraine, as it is immoral to aid and support insurgency, it's against democratic norm and principle hence one who believes in freedom would also abide and not harm someone else's peace, because allegedly Russian political brass was seen playing disruptive role in harming the Ukrainian internal peace thereby western countries imposition of sanction against Russia could possibly be justified.

However, these same western nations like "U.S. Britain, France and Germany" have an absolute indifferent attitude and unjust principles, in their foreign policies, when it comes to dealing with nations whose political leadership is non-abiding and not in friendly terms with the western powers. Here, I'm referring to the approach the U.S. and western European countries have towards the oil rich wealthy Islamic nations in the Arab world, the western media and press for several decades have been writing about and debating of the role of oil rich wealthy nation like "Qatar, Saudi-Arabia, Kuwait, these rich Arab nations have been for many years and decades been supporting, aiding and helping the Islamic fundamentalist forces, the countries like Qatar, Saudi-Arabia covertly or overtly been aiding the Sunni-Muslim fundamentalist forces with allege linked to the Sunni-Muslim jihadist forces, the same jihadist forces who practice destructions, here once again these serious charges of abating and supporting the Islamic jihadist forces by the oil rich Arab nations, are levelled by none other than the media and press of the western world as well as many western politicians and academicians.

Now, the question arises is that if these western nations like America, Britain, French, Germany, takes a lead and enforce economic sanctions against Vladimir Putin Russian government for its alleged role of supporting the rebel insurgent inside Ukraine, than, why these western countries are turning a blind eye to the intelligence reports as well as information from many other sources that the oil rich Arab nations are advertently helping and financing the terrorists. Why is the western countries not severing ties with countries like Qatar, Saudi Arabia and Kuwait?

Instead these western countries like US and its allies are strengthening relations with these Arab countries and funny as it may sound the US and its western European allies are making these oil rich Arab nations partner in their resolve to fight war on terror against the same terrorist group who are allegedly funded by these Arab nations.

Friends friend are our friend and friends foe are our foe, enemies enemy are friends, with regards to Syria how these western countries have contrarian approach and indifferent foreign policies, Syria is arguably the most adversely affect country in the so-called Arab spring Mid-east political crisis, here again it is worth mentioning the role of western countries double standard. Because the Syrian president "Bashar al-Assad" belonging to Shiite sect of Islam and because the western allies in the Arab region namely Qatar, Saudi, Kuwait belonging to Sunni sect, as well as Syrian president Assad being a close ally of Russia and Russia apparently an old foe and bitter rival of US and west-European nations, so, despite the fact the Syrian president Assad's secular and liberal credentials the western countries vehemently oppose him and vociferously demanded his ouster from power by siding with the Sunni terrorist group, quite evidently when it suit the purpose of the powerful western country at times they label even a terrorist group as moderates. The free Syrian army forces members who are fighting against the Syria president Assad army forces, this free Syrian army whom the French, Britain, and America are calling moderates and thereby aiding supporting and financing their militant operation, the members of free Syrian army are actually nobody else but they are mostly

Chechen mafia or terrorist from Chechnya and Afghanistan belonging to fundamentalist Sunni jihadist school of thoughts.

Syria is a multicultural and multi religious country with its citizens divided into many different big and small religious group, however even though Sunni-Muslim are the majority population in Syria, apparently it's only the Sunni sect that's fiercely been opposing and emphatically demanding the ouster of Syrian president Assad's regime, the other dozen or so religious community are either fully backing the Assad regime or at least not vocal in demanding the ouster Syrian president Assad from president-ship, hence being president of a country it is the constitutional duty of the head-of-state to defend the sovereignty of their country, that's exactly the Syrian president been doing fighting the unlawful elements and terrorist groups who are trying to capture power in Syria with selfish objective of decimating freedom and civil rights of its citizens and establishing 7th century barbaric Islamic Sharia law.

The otherwise strong advocates of democracies and preachers human rights, the western power instead of siding with the Syrian president and help him crush the Islamic fundamentalist forces, these western nations US and its crony nations are subtly and systematically helping the venomous Islamic forces.

To protect the sovereignty of their own country and for the safety of their citizens, the US, France, Britain, Israel, severely and ferociously hits out at the Islamic jihadist terrorist, the Israel battered Hamas militants in Gaza, US flies unmanned combat aircraft "Drone" to hit out at terrorist targets inside countries like Somalia, Yemen, Afghanistan and Pakistan, but the western countries takes strong exception when the Syrian president Assad army hits back at the terrorist camps.

In the 1980s the then Iraqi dictator and Al-Qaeda founder Osama were America's blue eyed boys, when Saddam was serving the purpose of the western countries when Saddam was at war with America's foe Iran and Saddam was providing commercial benefits to the western corporates and governments, at that point all of Iraqi dictator "Saddam's" ills were being ignored by the West, when Saddam's army dropped nerve gas chemical (chemical weapon) on the Northern-Iraqi Kurdish city of Halabja which reportedly killed 5000 Kurdish people, the western countries largely ignored to incident and mildly condemned the gruesome incident, U.S. largely maintained stoic silence over the incident.

Similarly, the US and it cronies and the US intelligence agency CIA supported and aided the Al Qaeda in the 1980s, the CIA supported Osama Bin Laden during the Soviet occupation of Afghanistan during the 1980s, at that time the US had believed that Al Qaeda and Taliban are moderate rebel fighters and will serve their purpose in fighting and defeating the Russian backed soviet army, because it wasn't in the strategic interest of the US for Russia to have a strategic control over Afghanistan.

The Al Qaeda terrorist even allegedly played crucial and decisive role in the ouster of Libyan dictator Gaddafi, in the year 2011, while British and French army forces Air-strikes aerial bombardment striking targets from air by dropping bombs on Gaddafi's army bases, it were the allege Al Qaeda terrorist who were fighting against the formidable army of Gaddafi on the ground, therefore the Al Qaeda's militants in a way helped those power who wanted to see Gaddafi dislodged from power of the oil rich country of Libya.

To alleviate the mighty power of Russia and to curb its control in global politics that of astute Russian president Vladimir Putin, the US and its intelligence agencies have not hesitated in taking help of Chechen mafia and Chechen terrorist.

The bonhomie between political class and terrorist continues, it's always give and take deal, the political bosses have to in some ways return favour to the terrorist, who many a times comes to the rescue of the political leadership. And the terrorist and mafias have to share a portion of the illegal income with voracious politicians as well as with the influential religious hierarchy (depending on the might of the political forces and strength of the religion in the area/areas the terrorist groups operates) to keep them in good humour.

So, not just the western countries like US, France, Britain but even other powerful nations like China and Russia do indulge in manoeuvring and resort to arm twisting depending on the vulnerability of the country they are dealing with, each of these powerful countries foreign policies are design selfishly to suit their purpose.

A very pressing question that does round in the minds of many us, as in, what is terrorism? Who are the terrorist?

Well, the terrorist have streamline and corporatize terrorism and terrorist activities, in old age terrorist were mainly unemployed, repressive, psychopath who use to take up arms in their hands and start killing people whom they use to perceive as their enemy or enemies of their region or religion.

Terrorism, mafia, warlords or smugglers, are basically same side of the same coin or two side of the same coin.

Terrorist and mafia activities are manifold, their activities includes killing, kidnapping, hijacking, narcotics drug trades, terrorism has become a global phenomenon.

But, sadly, whenever and whosoever talks of sleazy and wicked trade and terrorism, not surprising to many but they only talk of people who owes allegiance to Islam, the Islamist are branded as monsters as most people thinks the world over that terrorism is synonymous with Islamic folks, how rude of them, electronic as well as the print media also not to be left behind is the political fraternity have inadvertently or knowingly have played a crucial role in branding Islam as religion of destruction, almost every day it has become a norm that we see images of Islamic terrorist noxious activities at our home on TV sets, as well we read about Islamic terrorism in newspaper, true, we can't deny it nor am I denying it, because it's a fact, however, purpose behind is not to give Islamist people any clean chit, yes, without an iota of doubt there are many dreaded terrorists and terrorist groups which belongs too and practice Sunni-Islam, Islam is another name of destruction, but!

We must again be fair in our assessment of things, should not be discriminative and be harsh in criticism, it is unjust to simply brand Islam as religion of demon and debase Islamist people, and brazenly turn blind eye and ignore the brutal crimes that people of other faith and religions commits.

Do thorough reality check and there are radicals and smugglers in Europe as well, the most famous fraternity is the mafia of Sicily in Italy notoriously well known for committing heinous crimes, South America is Christian/Catholic dominated region of the world, the south-American Drug mafias, warlords and terrorism is as savage, cruel and ugly as perhaps Islamic terrorism of Arabian region is. The activity of the Latin terrorist or mafias in South-American countries like Brazil and Colombia, the notorious Mexico drug mafias and war lords notorious for their gang wars and political killings, not to be left behind arguably the most dangerous Latin country "Guatemala" According to New Yorker magazine, in 2009, fewer civilians were reported killed in the war zone of Iraq than were shot, stabbed, or beaten to death in Guatemala, and 97% of homicides "remain unsolved." The high rate of murder has been blamed on "a highly powerful criminal cartel", made up of politically connected retired military officers and linking with drug traffickers and other criminals. The main activities of the mafias and terrorist of the Latin American countries involves trading in narcotics drugs, political killings, kidnappings, human trafficking, sex slave, illegal betting on sports and match fixing.

Not far behind are the mafias and terrorist groups based in Africa, which includes both Muslims and Non-Muslims, their nefarious activities includes, killing of endangered animals and trade in illegal animal skin, trade in ivory, illegal mining of diamond and gold, as well as killing and human trafficking and slave trade, Pirates (looting ships).

To put things in better perspective in wider context; for example if in Christian dominated country like Mexico where if an outlawed miscreants and criminal gangs commits heinous crimes of brutal killings, kidnapping and massacring of innocent civilians, in which case it has been observed that the global media and almost all the governments around the world response is rather tepid or largely considered to be insignificant issue to be discussed or commented about hence such incidents of crimes in Mexico and Brazil are rarely discussed in mainstream media, but in contrast when Islamic people commits brutal inhuman crimes like bomb blast and massacres or beheadings in which case it becomes the most extensively covered news story almost instantly the media, be it, Electronic or Press (print – newspaper) will make crimes committed by

Muslims their top news story and will most prominently be presented in TV news reports and front page headline news in newspapers, also it be immediately be condemned by political leaderships from around the world and will become topic of discussion in social gatherings. Well, my friends will agree with me that there is a bi-polar division among citizens of our world on religious ground, our world community is outrageously and deeply communally polarized between Non-Muslims and Muslims.

Obvious fact is that, all five fingers of our hand is not of same size, but, yet, all five fingers are still part of our hand and have same roots connected to our nerve centre, so, crimes and terror of any kind and types in nature, crime is a crime no matter who commits it, "Muslims or Non-Muslims" whichever part of the world it happens, barbarism has to be condemned emphatically and comprehensively "**Period**" No ifs and No buts.

To understand more about terrorists and terrorism: Trading and dealing in counterfeit currencies and money laundering is part of every major or small "terrorist group and mafias" around the world.

With so many trade and business interest, No wonder, why terrorist organizations as well as the mafias have become diversified business conglomerate. Many corporates and leading multinational Banks secretly woos these terrorist and mafias to do business with them, particularly the illegal transfer of money and money laundering.

So, most trading activities even though illegitimate in nature, but, these terrorists and mafias and the smugglers need lots of manpower to run their illegal business activities, so quite obvious that these intimate terror organizations needs lots of manpower, but not only manpower, but they need highly skilled and proficient talented people to work for their organizations.

It has been reported that ISIS (Islamic state of Iraq and al-sham) terrorist group alone in worth over 2 billion US dollars, and ISIS earns approximately 5 million US dollars a day just from trading in illegal crude oil sales alone and much more cash from its other activities like kidnapping and ransoms.

This is precisely the reason, why joining terrorist groups or joining the mafias & smugglers have become a good career option for many ambitious youngsters, both gender male and females are these days not averse to the idea of joining and working for the terrorist groups or the smugglers and warlords.

The profession like "Terrorist, Mafia, Smugglers, Warlords" may be bad names for those who love peace and firmly believes in humanity, but these professions like terrorism has become like science, to operate terrorist group a lot of strategic planning is required, also required is fund mobilizations, workout deals and negotiate terms with politician and religious hierarchy, management of financial resources and managing media as well as recruiting the right skill workforce above all providing high skill training to the combative recruits, so all these makes managing terrorist organizational operation extremely challenging.

Some of the most establish terrorist groups like Al Qaeda, Boko Haram, ISIS, Taliban, have prospered and progressed because of highly oriented and well entrenched manpower, these groups allegedly had or have some of the most talented and skilled people working for them.

Again, what lures youths to join terrorist groups is obviously opportunity to earn good amount of money, also extra curricula fun like sex, drugs, action, adventure, free and good quality food, clothes and opportunity to travel to different places.

For some it would be surprising, but it's a fact, that these terrorist organizations hire and recruits professional from diverse fields, the terrorist groups and the mafias recruit brave heart and semi-skilled folks for combative operations and to intimidate people, then highly skilled professionals are recruited from the fields like Political science graduates for strategic & resource planning, then they need help from Graduates from Business and finance (MBA's) who have expertise in managing finances and mobilizing funds and money laundering, Public Relation (PR) is very important for the survival of the terrorist groups, as we are living in digital age, hence the role of social media becomes very important, especially the Islamic terrorist groups are making optimal use of social media network to forward there message and propagate there propaganda to the wide masses among the Muslim population and also to woo the potentially vulnerable from non-Muslim community, the social media network like "Facebook, You-tube, Twitter etc" are used by the jihadist to full extent to woo the non-Muslims to convert to Islam and to become jihadist, also the social media is extensively used by the terrorist to recruit the required members to join their terror organization, hence these terrorist groups nowadays hires most tech savvy individuals and individuals with good knowledge of sales and promotions so that these professionals can manage both traditional media and social media.

Also most important for these terrorist group is to hire the most experienced and skilled personnel who has expertise in strategic defence and military procedures, the mafias as well as terrorist groups needs highly talented persons who are from the field of combative defence service, hence many army deserters or former army/military commanders are either hired as consultants of recruited as full time members mostly by the organised terrorist groups and other outlawed rebel groups, for the purpose that these defence experts can help in sourcing much needed arms and ammunitions for the groups as well to train and to teach the combative terrorist forces to use and to operate arms for their combative missions.

Call it cybercrime or cyber terror, yes, cyber terror is another form of terror that can severely harm the country's infrastructure, the cyber terror can destroy banking and corporate functioning by transmitting virus or hacking their system, money can be siphoned off from bank accounts, cyber terror can throw the government departmental files and programme into tizzy. Yes, the cybercrime/cyber terror is very lethal weapon the terrorist groups and miscreants have which potentially can cause immense destruction.

Cybercriminals – Cyber Fraudsters – Cyber Terrorists; give them whatever name you like, call them by whatever name you want too, but the fact remains is that Criminals, gangsters, mafias and terrorist have kept pace with time and have institutionalized there wicked methods of committing Crimes. The new age crimes and corrupt practices of 21st century are increasingly becoming more and more advanced and sophisticated, be it small time petty criminals or more organized Mafia syndicates or the dreaded hard-core terrorist groups, they've all remarkably well upgraded their style of functioning and operating there criminal activities, New age criminals living with time have adopted more scientific advance technology to execute ideas of perpetrating crimes and terror.

The terrorist as well as the mafias like mixing business with pleasures hence they always woo young girls to join there group, so you'll find many beauties wandering around the terrorist bosses.

Chapter 8

Call spade a spade and call niggard a niggard, well, if we discuss Rape, Sex, Sex slave, Prostitutions or Force marriage, these are mostly female related issues, which are often discussed when the topic of Discrimination against women is debated.

No immoral man can ever succeed in his objective unless he obtains support of a selfish crafty woman. Woman is the best tool man can have, as it's always seen woman listens to woman and trust her and is least doubtful about her motives.

It has been observed that woman when she is frustrated and beleaguered, when she realizes that her life has been messed up or otherwise, these kind or type of women will always cleverly and systematically will make an attempt to ruin the life of other women as well, not all, but, some of the women whose life is in ruins and is grave disorder, "they think in their mind" this way, have a listen "if I am unhappy, if my life is messed up," then, why should others be happy?

It has been reported that even in terrorist groups, it is no other than the women terrorist members have taken over the responsibility of wooing and enticing other young women to join terrorist organization and luring credulous women to become jihadist and surrender their body for sex jihad. Here I would like to say that this doesn't relate to any particular religion but these are certain harsh realities of our society, woman being a woman it becomes easy for her to entice and lure other gullible women by speaking highly emotional rhetoric and enacting drama, to make other women agree to her suggestion of entering into sleazy relationship or joining intimate professions like terrorism, prostitutions or other types of illegal sleazy trade practice.

So, excruciating circumstances and when their life is in quandary, some of the women turn extremely cunning and callous.

Women in a role of "mother, sister or friend" can help other women by giving them wise advice, support them financially, give other women right guidance, a woman can and does do a lot of good and wonderful things for other women's welfare and benefits, but, on the flip side, a woman can under duress or frustration become "Lamia" and destroy other woman or women life and career beyond imagination.

So, it's rightly said, that, "**Women are women's best friends and their worse adversaries.**"

Women in her positive flavour is an exemplary example of forbearance and tolerance, but the reverse is the negative features of how women could prove to be extremely disruptive and destructionist.

Gracious woman obtains dignity while aggressive woman obtains wealth.

Domestic violence is a bigger menace than compare to terrorism or conventional military wars, yes, surprising, but this is what many research surveys and studies conducted by many human rights and civil liberties groups have found out that domestic violence is much more devastatingly harmful, troublesome and cost-wise as well very expensive than compare to terrorism or wars fought by military in the battlefields.

Domestic violence is gender and religion neutral, every section of the society affluent class or underclass could be affected, "Male or Female, Gay or Straight, Children or Senior Citizens," anyone of us across geographic and demographic could potentially become victim of domestic violence. Many cases of attempted suicides or actual suicides as well as people becoming drug addicts or alcoholics are also mostly those kind of people who've been victim of domestic violence.

Domestic violence victims suffers from extreme stress, as domestic violence stigmatize the person or persons affected by it. But, to put it in perspective and to define Domestic violence, its effects are both psychological and physical, it is unique in nature, as it happens in many different types and forms, apparently it's more subtle, at times it largely proves to be unfelt and unnoticed.

The figures show, however, that it consists mainly of violence by men against women. Children are also affected, both directly and indirectly and there is also a strong correlation between domestic violence and child abuse suggesting overlap rates of between 40-60%. Abusers are in control of themselves when they abuse? Despite what many people believe, domestic abuse is not due to the abuser's loss of control over his/her behaviour. Domestic abuse is a deliberate choice made by the abuser.

Here is a saying, "**When Dog bites a Man, it doesn't become a News, but, when Man bites the Dog, it becomes a Big News**," Ha-ha-ha, well jokes apart, I really mean it, when Man harass or humiliates woman it becomes a big issue, lots of people come forward to show their solidarity with the woman who has been harmed and suffered brutality of man's aggression, but, on the flip side when a Woman harass, hassles or exploits a Man or men's to gain undue favour or financial benefits, the dichotomy of the man is that he doesn't get enough support or sympathy from the section of the society when he is humiliated and mentally tortured by a woman, so, the law needs to be **Even** and there should be equal and fair justice for every human, whether Man or Woman each of them should be provided equal honour and dignity to live their life graciously, and none should be allowed to be exploited or discriminated.

Domestic violence — also called intimate partner violence; which occurs between people in an intimate relationship. Domestic violence can take many forms, including emotional, sexual and physical abuse and threats of abuse. Men are sometimes abused by partners, but domestic violence is most often directed towards women. Domestic violence can happen in heterosexual or same-sex relationships. It might not be easy to identify domestic violence at first. While some relationships are clearly abusive from the outset, abuse often starts subtly and gets worse over time. You might be experiencing domestic violence if you're in a relationship with someone who: "Calls you names, insults you or puts you down," "Prevents or discourages you from seeing family members or friends," "Tries to control how you spend money, where you go, what medicines you take or what you wear."

If you're lesbian, bisexual or transgender, you might also be experiencing domestic violence if you're in a relationship with someone who: "Threatens to tell friends, family, colleagues or community members about your sexual orientation or gender identity."

The migrant workers whether its men or women are more prone to domestic violence, when people migrate from rural part of their country to the big urban city or when people from third-world country migrate to prosperous developed countries in search for better and lucrative job opportunities and to seek high income jobs, most of these people at times become serious victim of hatred crimes or domestic violence, females have to largely suffer from excruciating sexual harassment while men migrant workers often suffers from mental torture and discriminations of various kinds, the migrant folks suffers such excruciating domestic violence and hatred crimes because they are someone who is strange in the big unknown town or city and often have no friends or relatives and are oblivious of the cities or the countries legal system, that's what makes the migrant workers more vulnerable to many different types of domestic violence related crimes.

If one fervently believes women should stay inside their homes and out of the business of public life, what better way to accomplish that than rampant sexual harassment and sexual assault in a country in which women's virginity and honour is the sine qua non of female participation in society?

What about the Burqa's Muslim women are forced to wear? The systematic executions of innocent Christian women for witchcraft in the Middle-Ages? The barring of women becoming Catholic priests? The polygamous lifestyle of Mormons? The "honour" executions of Muslim wives for any infraction to the patriarchal interpretation of the Quran? The horrific mutilations of female genitals practiced by religious figures in Central Africa and Middle East? It seems every world religion is intensely patriarchal. *Every one of them engages in the systematic devaluation of women, in the systematic exclusion of women from positions of authority, and in the systematic oppression and even enslavement of women. I have yet to find a single major religion that bucks this trend. Considering how little many of these religions have in common otherwise, this is a truly remarkable pattern.*

Repression and exploitation are different, but complementary, forms of control and abuse of female sexuality. Women and girls' sexuality is repressed by strict control on sexual activity through such customs as placing a premium on girls' virginity, basing family honour on the sexual control of daughters and wives, exacting severe punishment for adultery, preventing equal access to divorce, and segregating girls and women from boys and men. Patriarchal religions, which mould most of the cultures of the world, subordinate women and girls to men. Fundamentalist movements, whether Christian, Jewish, Hindu or Islamic, advocate the repression of women and girls' sexuality. Women and girls' interaction with men and boys is closely monitored and restricted and their bodies and hair covered in a way deemed to be modest. For example, under the influence of Islamic fundamentalism, women are required to wear full body coverings, such as chadors and Burqas. Punishment for sexual misconduct can be severe, as in Saudi Arabia, Afghanistan or Iran, where women can be legally stoned to death.

Female abuse is a common phenomenon that takes shape in several forms in societies. However this phenomenon tends to be extreme in certain communities, where women are mercilessly "Battered" by males of their household.

Definition of honour killing is when a family member, or clan member, takes the life of another family member (who has shamed the family) in order to restore honour to the family or clan. Both men and women are victims of honour killing, however, women tend to be the victim more often and it is common for younger brothers to commit the murder. These crimes happen because of cultural behaviour and how that society views acceptable and unacceptable behaviour. It is supported by fundamentalist who are in governing roles. There are no laws to protect the women. There are expectations within society that forces citizens to continue these crimes. If one attempts to challenge these practices, they will die.

The reasons that stand behind women "Battering" are many, some men beat women because they feel physically strong. Ironically this physical superiority is only displayed over females, almost never over other "Males."

Its widely perceived and believed that there is no document in the world that states that the "Male" is in anyway better than female, and such behaviour only reveals perverted traditions and Male insecurity.

Mother-hood is all about supreme sacrifice and benevolent, woman in a role of mother is to give her child the best care and loving experience, of course mothers do give a lot of love and affection to her children there are many exemplary examples you will find, but, with heavy heart I also have to mention that "**Not**" all mothers are the same, there are some demonising examples of how evil and life threatening a woman as mother can be or has proven to be.

There are women in this world (living or death) who in the role of mother have proved to be example of extreme selfishness and brutality. Covertly, overtly or subtly, Many mothers look in their children a potential benefit for themselves, particularly if they have a daughter, for many mothers they consider their daughters to be a money minting machine, yes, there are many mothers who sell their daughter/daughters or force their daughters into marriages for monetary gains, many mothers simply by persuasion or by exerting pressure forces their daughters into prostitution or in other intimate professions.

There are also many incidents and examples you'll find if reported criminal cases are studied wherein the mothers have been found accused of plotting to have murdered her daughter, yes 100% true, such murders/killings are often called Honour killings, well, if the books of registered criminal cases and media reports are opened you'll find millions of incidents that has happened over hundreds of years which accentuates the gruesome nature of humans misdemeanour, we people at times are not safe among our own people, sometimes the victim of domestic violence don't realize it at all, but, even if they do notice it, feel it, realize it, and are aware of the fact, as in, how we are being ill-treated or unfairly being dishonoured by our voracious family members or relatives, yet person who is suffering excruciating humiliation at home do not protest or open their mouth in public, instead, he/she tend to restrain him/herself and prefers to swallow the bitter pill.

How selfish our own family members can be or could be, mainly in Asian and African countries it will be found there are many examples, wherein in the family the woman or to say daughter of the house is the lone bread-winner or if the daughter is the prominent earner. In such a scenario, the parents or even the siblings of the woman who's the principle earning member of the house, this parents particularly the mother knowing how important is her daughter's monthly income for the survival of the family, in such types of cases the mothers very cleverly and subtly will exert emotional pressures on her daughter and will try to convince her daughter to differ her marriage plan if any she may have in her mind so that her family does not have to fall on hard times. Daughter being a daughter is often seen to be very considerate, many women from socially conservative communities mostly in countries from Asia and Africa taking into consideration the obligation they have towards their immediate family, such girls and women makes supreme sacrifice and puts on hold their search for spouse for themselves for indefinite period of time and prefers instead of growing older holding the hands of her parents rather than spouse, these beleaguered girls and women grows older becoming stick of their old-age parents.

So, as I mentioned earlier in one of the page of this book, that domestic violence is of many different types an forms, not just lower or middle-class families that are affected, in fact the elite and privilege class families are more severely affected by domestic violence and discriminations, large scale reports suggest about brutal incidents of bitter divorces, family break-ups, sibling rivalry, forgery, betrayal, suicides, violence and bickering happening mostly in rich and wealthy families in affluent neighbourhoods.

When others harm and hurt us, we lament a lot, but, when people are cheated by their own near and dear ones, when our own people and our own family members systematically exploits us, it shatters us emotionally, it is always going to be very frustrating and deeply depressing, will always be hard to come out of such a harrowing situation, because it's our own folks who have bitten us.

There is a famous saying; "Behind every successful Man there is a Woman," I would just like to twist the famous saying, please allow me to say it differently in my own way, have a listen; > "Behind the Pain and Agony of every Woman there is a woman."

The woman who does not require validation from anyone is the most feared individual on the planet.

So, be it, Eastern part of the World or Western part of the World, we humans have a lots in common among us. No matter what "Race or Religion" we belong too, per-se humans have common mentality.

It is always a women that you'll find is most religious, the female population of the world for ages have been devout religious and have repose unprecedented faith in the divine spirit and divine power, the women supports the founders of religious faith the most as compare to men and the women have been religiously following the teachings thought by the men who've founded particular religion, as compare to men, the women are always found to be more spiritual and religious, yet, Man being Man, as all the founders of every religion as well as the so-called holy-books are written by men.

The holy-books are nothing but proven to be outrageously un-holy for the women gender, the men's who have scripted their thoughts than branded and promoted their written so-called holy-books as message of god, these so-called holy books are abhorrently discriminating against women, every men who's written the so-called religious holy-book has simply hoodwink the common people into believing that their written holy-book has divine message in it and that reading their holy-book will help its followers and readers come out of crisis and will bring to them immense peace, wealth and prosperity.

So, what has these religions done for women? Yes, on the positive side many of the religions run religious institutions have been providing some amount of monetary help and shelters as well as supporting in empowering some women, but, as many astounding revelation and disclosures and investigation have found and indicated that most of the women are most humiliated and discriminated inside the corridors of these religious institutions by their religious or community hierarchy.

Islam ever since it emerged on global map as one of the most influential religion, Islamic belief and its followers overwhelmingly and disgracefully disregard and despise every other religions and religious beliefs, the Muslim folks mince no words in calling other religious and also the Non-believers atheist as infidels, hence the world which is so overwhelmingly divided and polarized between Muslims and non-Muslims, hence every aspect of Islamic teachings and preaching is thoroughly scrutinize, so is the plight of Muslim women is compared by the ordeal of non-Muslim women's.

Yes it is true that Muslim women for generations have been discriminated and humiliated, their religious beliefs has proved to be catalyst in giving the men of Muslim community enough apparatus and ammunition to browbeat and flogged their wives, daughters or even women from their neighbourhood, some of the social ills and gruesome crimes like stoning women to death if even allegedly found to have committed adultery or if found unfaithful to her husband, honour killing force marriage these are some of the brutal harassment and crime that the Muslim women have stomach for generations.

Now, the non-Muslim people seeing the plight and quandary of Muslim women have got an opportunity to mock and tease the Muslims, rightly so, if they see some inhuman crimes so pervasive in Muslim community they will obviously talk and taunt, but apart from Islam which other religion or even the atheist can say that there are no crimes of brutality committed in or within their community or fraternity, the brutal crimes committed within Islam and by the people of Islam is discussed and debated at every street corner and at coffee table by both the Muslims and non-Muslim people the world over, but, these non-Muslim people forget to look inwards at their own-self, the other big and prominent religions are no less cruel, if you look at and dig deep into history books you'll find brazen and blatant crimes and flagrant civil right violations committed in all the most prominent religions like Christianity, Buddhist or Hindus. The women and children in particular been as badly and inhumanly treated in other religions as they perhaps maybe treated in Islam.

There have been many astounding fact finding reports published about Christianity, the revelations and disclosures and crime investigations have revealed how hard pressed the women of Christian religions have been, the reports and investigations have pointed out the fact that in most Christian/catholic religious institutions and churches where the priest and Nuns are either gays and lesbians, the sexual indulgence between male priest and Nuns are all too common, abortions and child abuse of both boys and girls, senior and influential Nuns sexually exploits the beleaguered and under privileged and junior Nuns and women, likewise the male priest often have been found to have sexually exploited women as well as young men and boys. Many catholic priest go so far to demand that heads of convent makes Nuns sexually available for them--- "testament to hypocrisy in the name of celibate of priesthood,"--- many sexually active priest have left a trial of wounded women and fatherless progeny, thousands of girls and boys have been molested by priest.

These reports of widespread misdemeanour have surfaced from Italy to Ireland and India to Mexico in various medium alleging the atrocities and heinous brutal crimes and bizarre adventurous activity inside the Christian/catholic churches and religious institutions, both consensual sex between priest and Nuns or infancy adolescence boys and girls, or forceful sexual exploitations by the priest and nuns, like rape and molestation which apparently results in unwanted pregnancy and abortion.

Pope's apology: one among many apologies by Vatican, (well Popes of different generations have been apologizing in the past for many of the sins committed inside Christian religious institutes by senior or junior priest or council members), so did, "Pope Francis as well during his Sunday Angelus prayers in saint Peter's square at the Vatican in July-2014;" **"Pope Francis** told victims of sexual abuse by Roman Catholic clerics the Church should "weep and make reparation" for crimes he said had taken on the dimensions of a sacrilegious cult.

"For some time now I have felt in my heart deep pain and suffering," Pope Francis said in his strongest comments yet on the crimes, delivered in the homily of a Mass with adult victims on Monday. "So much time hidden, camouflaged with a complicity that cannot be explained until someone realized that Jesus was looking." He had said he would not tolerate abuse by clerics, which has been exposed in recent years in many European, American and Asian dioceses. Bishops would be held accountable if they shielded them."…………..

The Hindus are most notorious the world over for exploiting the women, in most religious places and Dharmashala (Spiritual Dwelling) women are sexually exploited, as Hinduism is divided into upper-caste and lower-caste, hence the so-called upper-caste Hindus particularly the Men have for generations been sexually exploiting the most vulnerable so-called lower-caste women and children, some of the most heart rending and harrowing crimes of sexual abuse and discriminations have been committed in Hinduism. Glance through any history books and you'll read many incidents of Hindu women (Particularly the lower-caste Hindu women) being disrobed and paraded Naked on streets and in villages in India.

It has and will always happen, the religious priest irrespective of any religion as well as political leaders, they appear in public wearing very humble and polite expressions, their motive and purpose will be to prove by their attributes that they are man of peace and integrity, love and prosperity, that they are born to serve the purpose of common man. But there is a darker and ugly side of them as well which has always proven to be difficult to distinguish.

According to many experts the Indian sub-continent which also includes countries like "India, Pakistan, Bangladesh, Nepal, Sri-Lanka and I would also add Afghanistan," these countries of the sub-continent have been considered to be the most dangerous place for women/girls. Structural discriminations, most of these countries have insufficient and inappropriate sanitation facility, lack of toilets and bathrooms makes it challenging for women's to maintain physical and personal hygiene, which apparently makes women more vulnerable to contracting diseases, there are more mobile phone connections in country like India than there are good functional toilets.

Prejudice against female girl child is rampant particularly in India, from the medieval era to the present time, the thought process of many people unfortunately have not changed with time, they still live with primitive mentality, and have appallingly insular and superstitious characteristic, most parents consider girl child to be born in their family as jinx, the parents consider the girl child to be a burden, in most of the Indian sub-continent countries, it doesn't matter whether in rural village or urban cities, the mentality of the people are the same, it also doesn't matter whether the family is illiterate or academically qualified in fact worse offenders and abusers of girl child's are the affluent class, Sex-selective abortions, illegal, yet staggeringly high. Each year, over 600,000 female foetus are selectively aborted in India. The wealthy and literates are the worst offenders, many of the parents shamelessly puts humanity to shame by their inhuman and most wickedest activity, some among many parents and grandparents of the infant girl child who dislikes or feel burdened by the birth of a girl child in their house, there are incidents reported which have discovered the truth that many parents and grandparents of the infant girl child they callously throw their new born girl child in the street corner Thrash-Bin or leave the infant girl child on the railway platform, but even more horrendous is that I've heard some incidents happening in India in past that many parents and grandparents supported by friends and relatives have committed the most heinous of the crimes wherein the newly born girl child have been smashed to death by the grinding stone.

Girls are seen by many Pakistanis as a greater economic burden as most women are not permitted to work and are considered to be the financial responsibility of their fathers, and later their husbands. A Pakistani family can be forced to raise more than one million rupees (11,700 dollars) to marry their daughter off. More than 1,000 infants — most of them girls — were killed or abandoned to die in Pakistan in year-2010 according to conservative estimates by the Edhi Foundation, a charity working to reverse the grim trend. Such are the heart wrenching facts of the atrocities and crimes of hatred and prejudiced. Women are discriminated otherwise all over the world but the discrimination of women in the Indian sub-continent and particularly in India is an exception.

It will always be difficult for common people to rightly distinguish between Good or the Bad Evil, so, it is just that odd risk that we have to take in our life of trusting a person or things.

Is life difficult? Yes indeed, this is a greatest truth, but there are people in this world who enjoy hardship, there are people who are not at all scared of difficulty and are confidently ready to meet and accept any and every challenge, then, there are also people who are extremely scared of difficulty and unable to cope with pressure situations, call them cowards if you like, but people who are scared of difficulty such people mostly prefer to stay in comfort zone and to ensure their safety they do not hesitate but are always ready to make ridiculous compromises to keep trouble away from them.

It's normal to feel apprehensive when you try doing something new and different or when you have to face new challenges. Stepping out of the comfort zones and making yourself uncomfortable taking few odd risk can potentially give big rewards. To achieve greater success in life a person needs to initially go through a difficult phase as it is in time of adversity people get great ideas and power to execute those great ideas, which ultimately gives major peace and self-satisfaction when that person gains incredibly higher success in life. So, this is what life is all about, we never know what the end consequences will be of what we intend doing today, it's just that we need to take decisions and make choices of doing things we want to do.

In life, worldwide most people overwhelmingly concentrates mainly on improving their vocabulary and perfecting communication skills, nothing wrong with it, yes, it is always good to have good communication skills and be a good orator, so, what's missing? Well, even more important is, which apparently, sadly, not many people around the world focuses on or bother about, which is developing good **Listening Skills**. Yes, the crux of most problems in the world for the mankind is because most people have rather poor and appalling Listening skills, bad listening characteristic and mannerism of humans can cause and is causing unprecedented and devastating long lasting pain in most us life. Bad listening skills confounds peculiar types of problems and differences of opinion among individuals, leads to arguments and relationships break-ups. The crux of **Domestic Violence** is because people are less attentive among themselves and do not adhere to and listen to each other properly. The effects of domestic violence can destroy professional careers. So, *domestic violence* harms professional as well as sex life.

Difficult people will always create difficult situations, at home or at workplace or for that matter even in social circle, "it will be better not to try and **reason** the **unreasonable** person," so, you need to have the right **temperament** to remain calm in pressure situation.

As it is said, that, *you be good to others expect others to be good to you.*

Have a assertive and positive approach, differences and contentious issues needs to be sorted out amicably through dialogue and cordial discussions, one very important lesson to learn in life is, never to **Argue**, *argument is worst form of violence*, arguments normally have devastating consequences, arguments destroys personal image and gives bad reputation, arguments strains relationships or even causes breakup of relationships, be it in personal life, professional or business life, also frequent arguments precipitates domestic violence as well workplace violence, so be better advised, **always avoid argument**.

We can always only listen to person talking and see his/her expression and body language, but, what we can't do is, that, we can't access the other persons thoughts, hence the person/persons we deal with, we have to just look at and take things at face value, it will always be impossible for us to understand as to what is it that's really going on in his/her mind.

Different individuals have different Perception and Conviction; Our Perceptions and Convictions are self-serving purpose for our betterment, but our perceptions and convictions at times proves to be self-defeating, more often than not our worse enemy can't harm us as much we harm our own-selves, it is just because some individuals don't learn to accept their mistakes and take blame for their misfortune on themselves, people have tendency of blaming others for their plight.

Maturity is not when we start thinking big things, it is when we start understanding small things.

Sometimes it is better to be kind than to be right. We do not need an intelligent mind that speaks, but a patient heart that listens.